GUM

Literary Analysis and Composition

Student Guide

3rd Edition

About K12 Inc.

K12 Inc., a technology-based education company, is the nation's leading provider of proprietary curriculum and online education programs to students in grades K–12. K[12] provides its curriculum and academic services to online schools, traditional classrooms, blended school programs, and directly to families. K12 Inc. also operates the K[12] International Academy, an accredited, diploma-granting online private school serving students worldwide. K[12]'s mission is to provide any child the curriculum and tools to maximize success in life, regardless of geographic, financial, or demographic circumstances. K12 Inc. is accredited by CITA. More information can be found at www.K12.com.

978-1-60153-479-8

Printed by Courier, Kendallville, IN, USA, May 2015, Lot 052015

Table of Contents

Student Guide
Lesson 1: Sentences

When you go to a birthday party, you usually know who the guest of honor is--the person celebrating the birthday, of course. And you know what happens at a birthday party. Every party needs at least one activity planned, and lots of parties have several--blowing out the candles, playing games, and opening presents.

Just as every birthday party needs at least one guest of honor, every sentence needs at least one subject. And, just as every birthday party needs at least one activity, every sentence needs at least one verb.

Lesson Objectives

- Identify complete sentences and sentence fragments.
- Identify subjects and verbs in natural and inverted order.
- Identify the subject of a sentence when the subject is not stated.

PREPARE

Approximate lesson time is 25 minutes.

Materials

For the Student

Optional

About Grade 8 Language Arts

BK English Language Handbook, Level I - pages L5-L26

Extra Practice Answers

BK English Language Handbook, Level I - page L27

Keywords and Pronunciation

complete predicate : includes all the words that tell what the subject is doing or that tell something about the subject

complete subject : includes all the words used to identify the person, place, thing, or idea that the sentence is about

compound subject : two or more subjects connected by *and* or *or* that have the same verb

compound verb : two or more verbs connected by *and* or *or* that have the same subject

inverted sentence order : sentence order in which the verb or part of the verb phrase appears before the subject

natural sentence order : sentence order in which the subject comes before the verb

predicate : the predicate tells something about the subject

sentence : a group of words that contains a subject and a verb and expresses a complete thought

sentence fragment : a group of words that does not express a complete thought

simple predicate : the main word or phrase in the complete predicate

simple subject : the main word in the complete subject

subject : a noun or pronoun that names whom or what a sentence is about

understood subject : a subject that is not directly expressed; common in imperative sentences (commands), in which the subject you is usually understood but not stated

verb : a word used to express an action or a state of being

verb phrase : a main verb plus one or more helping verbs

LEARN

Activity 1: Sentences *(Online)*

Activity 2: Sentences *(Offline)*

Instructions

A. Recognizing Sentences

On page L5, read about sentences and sentence fragments. Then do Check Your Understanding on page L6, items 1-5.

B. Subjects and Verbs

Read about complete subjects and simple subjects on pages L7-L12. Then do QuickCheck on page L14, items 1-5.

Note – For this exercise and for the rest of the GUM program, the terms *subject* and *verb* refer to the simple subject and simple predicate.

C. Verb Phrases

On pages L14-L16, read about verb phrases. Then do Check Your Understanding on page L16, items 1-5.

D. Compound Subjects and Compound Verbs

On page L18, read about compound subjects. Then do items 1-5 of Check Your Understanding on page L19. Read about compound verbs on page L20. Then complete items 1-5 of the Check Your Understanding exercise on pages L20-L21.

E. Natural and Inverted Order

Read about the position of subjects on pages L22-L23. Then practice what you've learned and do Check Your Understanding on page L24, items 1-5.

F. Understood Subjects

On pages L25-L26, read about understood subjects. Then complete Check Your Understanding on page L26, items 1-5.

G. Check Your Work

When you have finished, ask an adult to check your answers to these exercises.

H. Assessment

Go online to take the assessment.

ASSESS

Lesson Checkpoint: Sentences (*Online*)

It's time to check what you have learned. Go to the next screen to test your skills.

LEARN

Activity 3. Optional: Sentences *(Online)*

Student Guide
Lesson 2: Fragments

On your first visit to the Takeyerchances Video Store, you rent a movie. You watch the whole film, only to realize that the last 10 minutes are gone! Upset, you take the video back. Ever courteous, the clerk convinces you to give the store another chance, so you accept a free rental. That night, you discover that this video starts right in the middle and has no beginning!

Sentence fragments are like the rentals from the Takeyerchances Video Store. Used carelessly in writing, they annoy people!

Lesson Objectives

- Distinguish between sentence fragments and complete sentences.
- Recognize how to correct a clause fragment.
- Recognize how to correct a phrase fragment.

PREPARE

Approximate lesson time is 25 minutes.

Materials

For the Student

BK English Language Handbook, Level I - pages L257-L265

Optional

Extra Practice/Challenge Answers

Finding Sentence Fragments

BK English Language Handbook, Level I - page L266

Keywords and Pronunciation

clause : a group of words that has a subject and a verb
clause fragment : a subordinate clause standing alone as if it were a sentence
independent, or main, clause : a clause that can stand alone as a sentence because it expresses a complete idea
phrase : a group of related words that acts as a single part of speech
phrase fragment : a phrase standing alone as if it were a sentence
sentence : a group of words that contains a subject and a verb and expresses a complete thought
sentence fragment : a group of words that does not express a complete thought
subordinate, or dependent, clause : a clause that cannot stand alone as a sentence because it does not express a complete thought

LEARN

Activity 1: Fragments *(Offline)*

Instructions

A. Sentence Fragments

Read pages L257-L258 to learn about sentence fragments. Then do Check Your Understanding on page L259.

B. Phrase Fragments

Read pages L260-L261, which will tell you about phrase fragments. Then do two exercises: Check Your Understanding on page L262 and Connect to the Writing Process on page L262.

C. Clause Fragments

Read pages L263-L264, which will tell you how to identify clause fragments. Then do two exercises: Check Your Understanding on pages L264-L265 and Connect to the Writing Process on page L265.

D. Check Your Work

When you have finished, ask an adult to check your answers to these exercises.

E. Assessment

Go online to take the assessment.

ASSESS

Lesson Checkpoint: Fragments (*Online*)

It's time to check what you have learned. Go to the next screen to test your skills.

LEARN

Activity 2: Fragments *(Offline)*

Instructions

Extra Practice: If you had difficulty with the concepts in this lesson, or you did not pass the Lesson Assessment, do the Finding Sentence Fragments page.

When you have finished, use the Extra Practice/Challenge Answers page to check your answers to the exercise.

Challenge: If you passed the Lesson Assessment with flying colors, do the QuickCheck on page L266.
When you have finished, use the Extra Practice/Challenge Answers page to check your answers to the exercise.

Name Date

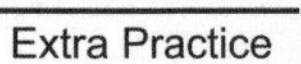

Finding Sentence Fragments

Finding Sentence Fragments *(pages L257–L258)* CHAPTER 9

EXERCISE **Identify each group of words as either a sentence or a sentence fragment.**

____ **1.** Plays piano very well.
A sentence
B fragment

____ **2.** My mother was playing the guitar.
A sentence
B fragment

____ **3.** The baby's toy is lost.
A sentence
B fragment

____ **4.** The baby's rubber toy.
A sentence
B fragment

____ **5.** The really interesting assembly yesterday.
A sentence
B fragment

____ **6.** We liked to rehearse before the assembly.
A sentence
B fragment

____ **7.** Walked all the way to the bus stop.
A sentence
B fragment

____ **8.** The children were finishing their tests.
A sentence
B fragment

____ **9.** The key was found in the kitchen.
A sentence
B fragment

____ **10.** The bottom drawer of the kitchen cabinet.
A sentence
B fragment

____ **11.** A young boy and girl.
A sentence
B fragment

____ **12.** He and I sang.
A sentence
B fragment

____ **13.** Ron liked to take a nap after lunch was over.
A sentence
B fragment

____ **14.** The fantastic lunch in the restaurant.
A sentence
B fragment

____ **15.** An hour and a half.
A sentence
B fragment

____ **16.** The team scored a run.
A sentence
B fragment

____ **17.** Scored a run after only six innings.
A sentence
B fragment

____ **18.** Please tie your shoe.
A sentence
B fragment

____ **19.** Heard a really good concert.
A sentence
B fragment

____ **20.** Cooked a terrific dinner this evening.
A sentence
B fragment

____ **21.** Red, purple, and blue are my favorite colors.
A sentence
B fragment

____ **22.** Wrote the word as clearly as possible.
A sentence
B fragment

Student Guide
Lesson 3: Run-ons

A new shipment of videos has arrived at the Takeyerchances Video Store. You decide to rent a film about Alaska. You start the movie and sit back. You're watching what you think is the last scene when suddenly the scene changes to Hawaii and new actors start talking! What's going on? You're confused. Is this new scene more of the movie, or is it another movie altogether?

This video is like a run-on sentence. It's confusing!

Lesson Objectives

- Distinguish between sentences and run-on sentences.
- Recognize how to correct a run-on sentence.

PREPARE

Approximate lesson time is 25 minutes.

Materials

For the Student

BK English Language Handbook, Level I - pages L267-L268

Optional

Extra Practice Answers

Run-on Sentences

Keywords and Pronunciation

complex sentence : a sentence that consists of one independent clause and one or more subordinate clauses
compound sentence : two or more simple sentences, joined by a comma and coordinating conjunction or by a semicolon
run-on sentence : two or more sentences that are written together and are separated by a comma or no mark of punctuation at all
sentence : a group of words that contains a subject and a verb and expresses a complete thought

LEARN

Activity 1: Run-ons *(Offline)*

Instructions

A. Run-on Sentences

On page L267, read about run-on sentences and how to correct them. Then, do two exercises: Check Your Understanding and Connect to the Writing Process, both on page L268.

B. Check Your Work

When you have finished, ask an adult to check your answers to these exercises.

C. Assessment

Go online to take the assessment.

ASSESS

Lesson Checkpoint: Run-ons (*Online*)

It's time to check what you have learned. Go to the next screen to test your skills.

LEARN

Activity 2: Run-ons *(Online)*

Name ______________________ Date ______________________

Extra Practice

Run-on Sentences

CHAPTER 9 Run-on Sentences *(pages L267–L268)*

EXERCISE A Decide whether each word group is a sentence or a run-on sentence.

____ **1.** Armon has several pets they include two turtles and one hamster.
A sentence
B run-on

____ **2.** Those earrings are unusual, they are made of genuine jade.
A sentence
B run-on

____ **3.** The dance will be held at the Robinsons' barn, which is just off Old Raven Road.
A sentence
B run-on

____ **4.** I took skiing lessons the instructor has been skiing since she was three years old.
A sentence
B run-on

____ **5.** When you entered the room, did you notice the painting on the wall?
A sentence
B run-on

____ **6.** I have three favorite subjects they are French, history, and chorus.
A sentence
B run-on

____ **7.** Just as I was getting comfortable, my mother called me to do the dishes.
A sentence
B run-on

____ **8.** Have you ever ridden on a roller coaster, my cousin just loves them.
A sentence
B run-on

____ **9.** I have three brothers two of them are in college.
A sentence
B run-on

____ **10.** As long as you're going to the kitchen, please get me an apple.
A sentence
B run-on

Student Guide
Lesson 4: Review

In this lesson, you will answer some review questions on what you learned in this unit about sentences. Before you take the Unit Assessment, this is your chance to find out what you do and don't know about sentences, subjects and verbs, sentence fragments, and run-on sentences.

Lesson Objectives

- Distinguish among complete sentences, sentence fragments, and run-on sentences.
- Identify subjects and verbs in sentences in natural and inverted order.
- Identify the subject of a sentence when the subject is not stated.
- Recognize how to correct sentence fragments and run-on sentences.

PREPARE

Approximate lesson time is 25 minutes.

Materials

For the Student

BK English Language Handbook, Level I - pages L28-L30 and page L271

Optional

Extra Practice Answers

BK English Language Handbook, Level I - pages L34-L35 and L274-L275

Keywords and Pronunciation

clause fragment : a subordinate clause standing alone as if it were a sentence

complete predicate : includes all the words that tell what the subject is doing or that tell something about the subject

complete subject : includes all the words used to identify the person, place, thing, or idea that the sentence is about

compound subject : two or more subjects connected by *and* or *or* that have the same verb

compound verb : two or more verbs connected by *and* or *or* that have the same subject

inverted sentence order : sentence order in which the verb or part of the verb phrase appears before the subject

natural sentence order : sentence order in which the subject comes before the verb

phrase fragment : a phrase standing alone as if it were a sentence

predicate : the predicate tells something about the subject

run-on sentence : two or more sentences that are written together and are separated by a comma or no mark of punctuation at all

sentence : a group of words that contains a subject and a verb and expresses a complete thought

sentence fragment : a group of words that does not express a complete thought

simple predicate : the main word or phrase in the complete predicate

simple subject : the main word in the complete subject

subject : a noun or pronoun that names whom or what a sentence is about

understood subject : a subject that is not directly expressed; common in imperative sentences (commands), in which the subject you is usually understood but not stated
verb : a word used to express an action or a state of being
verb phrase : a main verb plus one or more helping verbs

LEARN

Activity 1: Sentences, Fragments, Run-ons *(Offline)*

Instructions

A. Review

To prepare for the Unit Assessment, read about diagraming subjects and verbs on pages L28-L29. Then complete Practice Your Skills on page L29 of the handbook. Next do Finding Subjects and Verbs in the CheckPoint exercise on page L30, and the Correcting Sentence Fragments and Run-on Sentences in the CheckPoint exercise on page L271.

B. Check Your Work

When you have finished, have an adult check your answers. Make sure you understand the corrections for any mistakes you made. If you do that, then you should be ready for the Unit Assessment.

Activity 2: Sentences, Fragments, Run-ons *(Offline)*

Instructions

Complete the Posttest exercises on pages L34-L35 and L274-L275.

When you have finished, use the Extra Practice Answers page and check your answers.

Student Guide
Lesson 5: Assessment

Lesson Objectives

- Distinguish between sentence fragments and complete sentences.
- Distinguish between sentences and run-on sentences.
- Identify subjects and verbs in sentences in natural and inverted order.
- Identify the subject of a sentence when the subject is not stated.
- Recognize how to correct a run-on sentence.
- Recognize how to correct sentence fragments and run-on sentences.

PREPARE

Approximate lesson time is 25 minutes.

ASSESS

Unit Checkpoint: Sentences, Fragments, and Run-ons (*Online*)

It's time to check what you have learned. Go to the next screen to test your skills.

Student Guide
Lesson 1: Direct Objects and Indirect Objects

Picture this: As you walk through the door of your home, your brother passes you by and whispers, "I told." Your mind races through your recent mistakes--breaking a glass, spilling orange juice on the rug, and losing your allowance. Unfortunately, your brother didn't tell you *what* he told. And he didn't say *to whom*.

Too bad that your brother didn't complete his thought. That's what direct objects and indirect objects do. They complete the thought in a sentence.

Lesson Objectives

- Distinguish between direct and indirect objects in sentences.
- Identify direct objects in sentences.
- Identify indirect objects in sentences.

PREPARE

Approximate lesson time is 25 minutes.

Materials

For the Student

BK English Language Handbook, Level I - pages L149-L153

Optional

Direct and Indirect Objects

Extra Practice Answers

Keywords and Pronunciation

action verb : a verb that tells what action a subject is performing
adjective : a word that modifies, or describes, a noun or pronoun
adverb : a word that modifies a verb, an adjective, or another adverb
complement : a word that helps complete the meaning of a verb
compound direct object : two or more direct objects following the same verb
compound indirect object : two or more indirect objects following the same verb
direct object : a noun or pronoun that answers the question *What?* or *Whom?* after an action verb
indirect object : a noun or pronoun that answers the question *To or for whom?* or *To or for what?* after an action verb
modifier : a word or phrase that describes or changes another word's or phrase's meaning
predicate adjective : an adjective that follows a linking verb and modifies, or describes, the subject
predicate nominative : a noun or pronoun that follows a linking verb and identifies, renames, or explains the subject
prepositional phrase : a group of words that begins with a preposition, ends with a noun or pronoun, and is used as an adjective or adverb
sentence base : the basic parts of a sentence--the subject, verb, and complement

LEARN

Activity 1: Direct Objects and Indirect Objects *(Online)*

Activity 2: Direct Objects and Indirect Objects *(Offline)*

Instructions

A. Direct Objects

Read about direct objects on pages L149-L150 in the *BK English Language Handbook.* Then do Check Your Understanding on pages L150-L151.

B. Indirect Objects

Read about indirect objects on pages L151-L152. Then do two exercises: Check Your Understanding on page L153 and Connect to the Writing Process on the same page.

C. Check Your Work

When you have finished, ask an adult to check your answers to these exercises.

D. Assessment

Go online to take the assessment.

ASSESS

Lesson Checkpoint: Direct Objects and Indirect Objects (*Online*)

It's time to check what you have learned. Go to the next screen to test your skills.

LEARN

Activity 3. Optional: Direct Objects and Indirect Objects *(Online)*

Name ______________________________ Date ______________________________

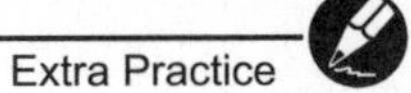
Extra Practice

Direct and Indirect Objects

Direct and Indirect Objects *(pages L149–L152)* CHAPTER 6

EXERCISE **Decide whether each underlined word is a direct object, indirect object, or neither.**

____ **1.** Wilbur Wright made his first famous flight in 1903.
A direct object
B indirect object
C neither

____ **2.** Then his brother Orville had accompanied him.
A direct object
B indirect object
C neither

____ **3.** Five years later he gave a friend a two-minute ride.
A direct object
B indirect object
C neither

____ **4.** As a result the friend became the first female airplane passenger.
A direct object
B indirect object
C neither

____ **5.** Before takeoff from Auvers, France, Mrs. Hart O. Berg prepared herself and her clothing for the rough ride.
A direct object
B indirect object
C neither

____ **6.** She tied her hat onto her head with a scarf.
A direct object
B indirect object
C neither

____ **7.** With a cord she gathered her full skirt around her ankles.
A direct object
B indirect object
C neither

____ **8.** As a result the wind would not blow her skirt or entangle it in the controls.
A direct object
B indirect object
C neither

____ **9.** After the short flight, Mrs. Berg walked away from the plane.
A direct object
B indirect object
C neither

____ **10.** She left the scarf on her hat and the cord on her skirt.
A direct object
B indirect object
C neither

____ **11.** French observers admired her idea and adopted the new fashion.
A direct object
B indirect object
C neither

____ **12.** Fashionable Frenchwomen sent their dressmakers new orders for such skirts.
A direct object
B indirect object
C neither

____ **13.** Parisian designers embraced the new style.
A direct object
B indirect object
C neither

____ **14.** Mrs. Berg had created the "hobble skirt."
A direct object
B indirect object
C neither

Student Guide
Lesson 2: Predicate Nominatives and Predicate Adjectives

If you needed a shirt, you wouldn't just call the store and say, "Send me a shirt." Who knows what you'd get! Instead, you'd name the brand and the style; you'd describe the color, the sleeve length, the size, and more. You'd say exactly what that shirt should *be*.

That's what predicate nominatives and predicate adjectives do. They rename or describe.

Lesson Objectives

- Distinguish between predicate nominatives and predicate adjectives in sentences.
- Identify predicate adjectives in sentences.
- Identify predicate nominatives in sentences.

PREPARE

Approximate lesson time is 25 minutes.

Materials

For the Student

BK English Language Handbook, Level I - pages L154-L158

Optional

Extra Practice Answers

Finding Linking Verbs and Subject Complements

Keywords and Pronunciation

compound predicate adjective : two or more predicate adjectives following the same linking verb, joined by a conjunction

compound predicate nominative : two or more predicate nominatives following the same linking verb, joined by a conjunction

direct object : a noun or pronoun that answers the question *What?* or *Whom?* after an action verb

indirect object : a noun or pronoun that answers the question *To or for whom?* or *To or for what?* after an action verb

linking verb : a verb that links the subject with another word that renames or describes the subject

predicate adjective : an adjective that follows a linking verb and modifies, or describes, the subject

predicate nominative : a noun or pronoun that follows a linking verb and identifies, renames, or explains the subject

prepositional phrase : a group of words that begins with a preposition, ends with a noun or pronoun, and is used as an adjective or adverb

subject complement : a word that identifies, renames, or explains the subject; includes predicate nominatives and predicate adjectives

LEARN

Activity 1: Predicate Nominatives and Predicate Adjectives *(Offline)*

Instructions

A. Predicate Nominatives

Read about predicate nominatives on pages L154-L155. Then do Check Your Understanding on pages L155-L156.

B. Predicate Adjectives

Read about predicate adjectives on pages L156-L157. Then do Check Your Understanding on pages L157-L158. Next, do Connect to the Writing Process on page L158.

C. Check Your Work

When you have finished, ask an adult to check your answers to these exercises.

D. Assessment

Go online to take the assessment.

ASSESS

Lesson Checkpoint: Predicate Nominatives and Predicate Adjectives (*Online*)

It's time to check what you have learned. Go to the next screen to test your skills.

LEARN

Activity 2. Optional: Predicate Nominatives and Predicate Adjectives *(Online)*

Name Date

Extra Practice 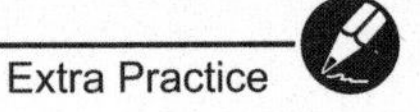

Finding Linking Verbs and Subject Complements

I. Select the correct linking verb and predicate nominative pair in each sentence.

1. Ms. Nobles was my voice teacher for two years.
   A. was, teacher
   B. was, years
   C. for, two
   D. for, years

2. Mr. Lee is my coach this year, and he can be tough.
   A. is, my
   B. is, coach
   C. can be, he
   D. can be, tough

3. Mark Twain became a popular writer who wrote many classics.
   A. became, popular
   B. became, writer
   C. wrote, many
   D. wrote, classics

4. Samuel Clemens was his real name.
   A. Samuel Clemens, was
   B. Samuel Clemens, name
   C. was, real
   D. was, name

5. Leonard Bernstein was a fine pianist in his day.
   A. Bernstein, pianist
   B. was, fine
   C. was, pianist
   D. was, day

Extra Practice 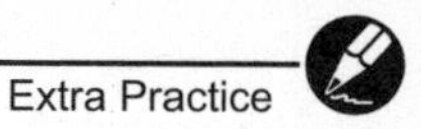

Finding Linking Verbs and Subject Complements

II. Select the correct linking verb and predicate adjective pair in each sentence.

6. A funnel will always be conical in shape.
   A. will always, shape
   B. will be, shape
   C. will be, conical
   D. will always be, shape

7. The ears and legs of a hare are relatively long.
   A. are, relatively
   B. are relatively, long
   C. relatively, long
   D. are, long

8. The city of Mecca in Saudi Arabia is holy to Muslims.
   A. is, holy
   B. is, Saudi Arabia
   C. is, Saudi Arabia, holy
   D. is, Muslims

9. Their car appears new after a fresh coat of paint.
   A. appears, paint
   B. appears, coat
   C. appears, fresh
   D. appears, new

10. Our basement usually remains cool and is a nice place for relaxation during the summer.
   A. remains, nice
   B. remains, cool
   C. remains, place
   D. is, nice

Student Guide
Lesson 3: Review

In this lesson, you will answer some review questions on what you learned in this unit about complements. Before you take the Unit Assessment, this is your chance to find out what you do and don't know about direct objects, indirect objects, predicate nominatives, and predicate adjectives.

Lesson Objectives

- Distinguish among the four kinds of complements.

PREPARE

Approximate lesson time is 25 minutes.

Materials

For the Student

BK English Language Handbook, Level I - pages L160-L165

Optional

Extra Practice Answers

BK English Language Handbook, Level I - pages L168-L169

Keywords and Pronunciation

action verb : a verb that tells what action a subject is performing
complement : a word that helps complete the meaning of a verb
compound direct object : two or more direct objects following the same verb
compound indirect object : two or more indirect objects following the same verb
direct object : a noun or pronoun that answers the question *What?* or *Whom?* after an action verb
indirect object : a noun or pronoun that answers the question *To or for whom?* or *To or for what?* after an action verb
linking verb : a verb that links the subject with another word that renames or describes the subject
predicate adjective : an adjective that follows a linking verb and modifies, or describes, the subject
predicate nominative : a noun or pronoun that follows a linking verb and identifies, renames, or explains the subject
prepositional phrase : a group of words that begins with a preposition, ends with a noun or pronoun, and is used as an adjective or adverb
sentence base : the basic parts of a sentence--the subject, verb, and complement

LEARN

Activity 1: Complements *(Offline)*

Instructions

A. Review

To prepare for the Unit Assessment, read Sentence Patterns on page L160 and do Practice Your Skills on page L161, items 1-10. Then read about diagraming complements on pages L162-L163 and diagram the sentences in Practice Your Skills on page L163. Next, complete both Identifying Complements exercises in CheckPoint on pages L164-L165.

B. Check Your Work

When you have finished, have an adult check your answers. Make sure you understand the corrections for any mistakes you made. If you do that, then you should be ready for the Unit Assessment.

Activity 2. Optional: Complements *(Offline)*

Instructions

Extra Practice: Complete the Posttest exercise on pages L168-L169.

When you have finished, use the Extra Practice Answers page and check your answers.

Student Guide
Lesson 4: Assessment

Lesson Objectives

- Distinguish among the four kinds of complements.
- Identify direct objects in sentences.
- Identify indirect objects in sentences.
- Identify predicate adjectives in sentences.
- Identify predicate nominatives in sentences.

PREPARE

Approximate lesson time is 25 minutes.

ASSESS

Unit Checkpoint: Complements (*Online*)

It's time to check what you have learned. Go to the next screen to test your skills.

Student Guide

Lesson 1: Prepositional Phrases

Just think of all the money your family could save if everyone wore a uniform! After all, why bother with all those colors, cuts, and sizes when one uniform could fit all? What? You wouldn't like it? You think clothes should be tailored to suit each person's size and personality?

Well, if you want clothes or anything else to fit a special situation, you need modifiers like prepositional phrases . You'll need adjective phrases to describe *which one* and *what kind*. And you'll need adverb phrases to tell *where, when, how, to what extent,* and *to what degree.*

Lesson Objectives

- Distinguish between adjective and adverb phrases in sentences.
- Identify adjective phrases and the words they modify in sentences.
- Identify adjective phrases in sentences.
- Identify adverb phrases and the words they modify in sentences.
- Identify adverb phrases in sentences.
- Punctuate adverb phrases correctly.

PREPARE

Approximate lesson time is 25 minutes.

Materials

For the Student

BK English Language Handbook, Level I - pages L173-L179

Optional

- Adjective Phrases
- Adverb Phrases
- Extra Practice Answers

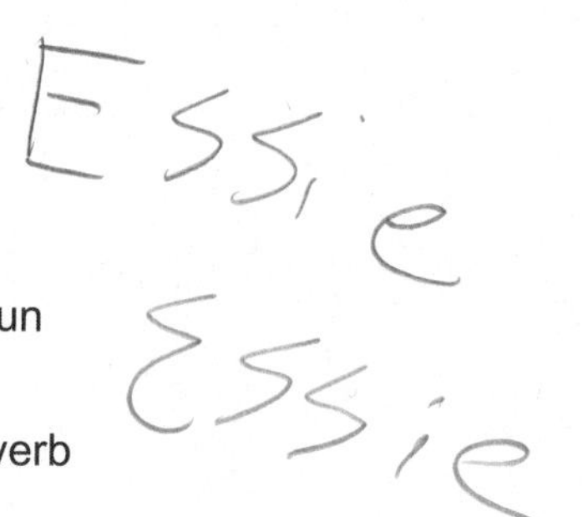

Keywords and Pronunciation

adjective : a word that modifies, or describes, a noun or pronoun
adjective phrase : a prepositional phrase that modifies a noun or pronoun
adverb : a word that modifies a verb, an adjective, or another adverb
adverb phrase : a prepositional phrase that is used mainly to modify a verb
noun : a word that names a person, place, thing, or idea
phrase : a group of related words that acts as a single part of speech
preposition : a word that shows the relationship between a noun or a pronoun and another word in the sentence
prepositional phrase : a group of words that begins with a preposition, ends with a noun or pronoun, and is used as an adjective or adverb
pronoun : a word that takes the place of one or more nouns
verb : a word used to express an action or a state of being

LEARN

Activity 1: Prepositional Phrases *(Online)*

Activity 2: Prepositional Phrases *(Offline)*

Instructions

A. Adjective Phrases

Read about prepositional phrases on page L173 and adjective phrases on pages L174-L175. Then, do Check Your Understanding on page L175.

B. Adverb Phrases

Read about adverb phrases and the punctuation of these phrases on pages L176-L178. Then do Check Your Understanding on page L178 and Connect to the Writing Process on page L179.

Note: For Connect to the Writing Process, you do not need to write the entire sentence. You may write only the word that should be followed by a comma.

C. Check Your Work

When you have finished, ask an adult to check your answers to these exercises.

D. Assessment

Go online to take the assessment.

ASSESS

Lesson Checkpoint: Prepositional Phrases (*Online*)

It's time to check what you have learned. Go to the next screen to test your skills.

LEARN

Activity 3. Optional: Prepositional Phrases *(Online)*

Name ______________________ Date ______________________

Extra Practice 

Adjective Phrases

Adjective Phrases *(pages L174–L175)* CHAPTER 7

EXERCISE Choose the adjective phrase or phrases in each sentence.

____ **1.** The gray cat on the welcome mat is sleeping.
A gray cat
B on the welcome mat
C is sleeping

____ **2.** Chess is the name of the game store I work at.
A Chess is the name
B of the game store
C I work at

____ **3.** The orange sweater in the closet is Kevin's.
A orange
B in the closet
C is Kevin's

____ **4.** The sailors told tall tales about faraway places.
A The sailors told
B told tall tales
C about faraway places

____ **5.** The film on the television was interrupted by a news brief.
A on the television
B was interrupted
C by a news brief

____ **6.** The aorta is an essential part of the heart.
A The aorta is
B an essential part
C of the heart

____ **7.** In the Senate, sixteen is the minimum age for a page.
A In the Senate
B sixteen is the minimum
C for a page

____ **8.** A frog in the swamp croaked loudly all night long.
A in the swamp
B croaked loudly
C all night long

____ **9.** That dish in the glass platter is not so tasty.
A That dish
B in the glass platter
C not so tasty

____ **10.** The dog in the kennel was happy to see his owners.
A in the kennel
B was happy
C to see his owners

____ **11.** The radio in the kitchen doesn't work.
A The radio
B doesn't work
C in the kitchen

____ **12.** The last twenty minutes of the movie at Cinema I was dull.
A of the movie
B at Cinema I
C of the movie, at Cinema I

____ **13.** None of the Pilgrims on the Mayflower had a middle name.
A on the Mayflower
B of the Pilgrims, on the Mayflower
C a middle name

____ **14.** The captain of the debating team met the principal.
A of the debating team
B the principal
C The captain

Name ___ Date ___

Extra Practice

Adverb Phrases

CHAPTER 7 Adverb Phrases *(pages L176–L178)*

EXERCISE **Select the adverb phrase or phrases in each sentence.**

___ **1.** Stu and Amy will meet at the corner.
A will meet
B at the corner

___ **2.** They will meet at noon.
A at noon
B meet at

___ **3.** Ken is travelling by train.
A by train
B travelling by

___ **4.** Mrs. Ricci drove to the soccer game.
A soccer game
B to the soccer game

___ **5.** She drove with great care.
A She drove
B with great care

___ **6.** She drove in the afternoon.
A drove in the afternoon
B in the afternoon

___ **7.** A cricket chirps with its legs.
A A cricket chirps
B with its legs

___ **8.** The steep trail goes to the mountaintop.
A goes to the mountaintop
B to the mountaintop

___ **9.** Before dawn the storm began.
A Before dawn
B the storm began

___ **10.** Into the tree crashed the boulder.
A Into the tree
B crashed the boulder

___ **11.** Hockey pucks are kept in a refrigerator before a game.
A pucks are kept
B in a refrigerator, before a game

___ **12.** A blue whale may weigh 5,000 pounds at birth.
A at birth
B 5,000 pounds

___ **13.** Since Wednesday we have been rehearsing the play.
A have been rehearsing
B Since Wednesday

___ **14.** The band performed on the field during halftime.
A on the field, during halftime
B band performed

___ **15.** A small boy on the riverbank fished for trout.
A on the riverbank
B for trout

___ **16.** During the winter a person cannot catch a cold at the North Pole.
A catch a cold
B During the winter, at the North Pole

___ **17.** I am very happy about your promotion.
A very happy about
B about your promotion

___ **18.** A bird sees everything at once in total focus.
A in total focus
B at once, in total focus

___ **19.** During the marathon we sat on the curbstone.
A During the marathon, on the curbstone
B we sat

___ **20.** Some lizards can run on their hind legs.
A on their hind legs
B Some lizards

Student Guide
Lesson 2: Misplaced Modifiers and Appositives

"What? What's that? I can't hear you. You're fading out. Did you say you want a poodle?" you yell into the cell phone.

"No! Get noodles, PASTA for soup!" your mother shouts and hangs up. You hang up, look at the cell phone, and wonder what your mother wanted you to buy.

In writing, a misplaced modifier is worse than a crackling phone line. Even an appositive or an appositive phrase might not make your meaning clear.

Lesson Objectives

- Identify appositives and appositive phrases and the words they rename in sentences.
- Identify appositives and appositive phrases in sentences.
- Identify misplaced modifiers in sentences.
- Punctuate appositives and appositive phrases correctly.

PREPARE

Approximate lesson time is 25 minutes.

Materials

For the Student

BK English Language Handbook, Level I - pages L180-L185

Optional

Appositives and Appositive Phrases

Extra Practice Answers

Keywords and Pronunciation

appositive : a noun or pronoun that identifies or explains another noun or pronoun in the sentence

appositive phrase : an appositive and its modifiers

misplaced modifier : a word or phrase that seems to modify the wrong word or words because it is too far from what it describes

---

LEARN

Activity 1: Misplaced Modifiers and Appositives *(Offline)*

Instructions

A. Misplaced Modifiers

Read about misplaced modifiers on pages L180-L181. Then do Check Your Understanding on page L181 and Connect to the Writing Process on page L182.

B. Appositives and Appositive Phrases

Read about appositives and appositive phrases on pages L183-L184. Then do Check Your Understanding on page L184 and Connect to the Writing Process on page L185.

Note: For Connect to the Writing Process, you do not have to write the entire sentence. You may write only the word or words that are followed by a comma.

C. Check Your Work

When you have finished, ask an adult to check your answers to these exercises.

D. Assessment

Go online to take the assessment.

ASSESS

Lesson Checkpoint: Misplaced Modifiers and Appositives (*Online*)

It's time to check what you have learned. Go to the next screen to test your skills.

LEARN

Activity 2. Optional: Misplaced Modifiers and Appositives *(Online)*

Name ______________________ Date ______________________

Extra Practice

Appositive and Appositive Phrases

Appositives and Appositive Phrases

(pages L183–L185)

EXERCISE **Select the noun that the underlined appositive or appositive phrase modifies.**

____ **1.** My friend Jason eats yogurt with raisins every day.
A friend
B yogurt
C raisins
D day

____ **2.** The poet Emily Dickinson spent all her life in the same house.
A poet
B spent
C life
D house

____ **3.** Elizabeth, the Queen of England, has four children.
A Elizabeth
B has
C four
D children

____ **4.** I met Mrs. Kolba, my English teacher, on the way to school.
A I
B Mrs. Kolba
C way
D school

____ **5.** Francis liked his birthday present, a pair of ice skates.
A Francis
B his
C birthday
D present

____ **6.** Cockroaches, those troublesome insects, are found all over the world.
A Cockroaches
B found
C all
D world

____ **7.** Denver, the capital of Colorado, is also its largest city.
A Denver
B also
C its
D city

____ **8.** The phone call was from Marshall, my sister's friend.
A phone
B call
C was
D Marshall

____ **9.** A good basketball player, Carla practices every day.
A Carla
B practices
C every
D day

____ **10.** I read two poems by the poet Robert Frost this week.
A two
B poems
C poet
D week

Student Guide
Lesson 3: Review

In this lesson, you will answer some review questions on what you learned in this unit about phrases. Before you take the Unit Assessment, this is your chance to find out what you do and don't know about adjective phrases, adverb phrases, misplaced modifiers, appositives, and appositive phrases.

Lesson Objectives

- Distinguish among adjective, adverb, and appositive phrases in sentences.
- Identify adjective, adverb, and appositive phrases and the words they modify or rename in sentences.
- Identify misplaced modifiers in sentences.

PREPARE

Approximate lesson time is 25 minutes.

Materials

For the Student

- Combining Sentences Using Appositive Phrases
- Identifying Phrases

Optional

- Extra Practice Answers
- Identifying Types of Phrases

Keywords and Pronunciation

adjective : a word that modifies, or describes, a noun or pronoun
adjective phrase : a prepositional phrase that modifies a noun or pronoun
adverb : a word that modifies a verb, an adjective, or another adverb
adverb phrase : a prepositional phrase that is used to modify a verb, adjective, or adverb
appositive : a noun or pronoun that identifies or explains another noun or pronoun in the sentence
appositive phrase : an appositive and its modifiers
misplaced modifier : a word or phrase that seems to modify the wrong word or words because it is too far from what it describes
noun : a word that names a person, place, thing, or idea
phrase : a group of related words that acts as a single part of speech
preposition : a word that shows the relationship between a noun or a pronoun and another word in the sentence
prepositional phrase : a group of words that begins with a preposition, ends with a noun or pronoun, and is used as an adjective or adverb
pronoun : a word that takes the place of one or more nouns
verb : a word used to express an action or a state of being

LEARN

Activity 1: Phrases *(Offline)*

Instructions

A. Review

To prepare for the Unit Assessment, read about Diagraming Phrases on pages L208-L209 and diagram the sentences in Practice Your Skills on page L209. Then print and complete the Identifying Phrases page and the Combining Sentences Using Appositive Phrases page.

B. Check Your Work

When you have finished, have an adult check your answers. Make sure you understand the corrections for any mistakes you made. If you do that, then you should be ready for the Unit Assessment.

Activity 2. Optional: Phrases *(Offline)*

Instructions

Extra Practice: Complete the Identifying Types of Phrases page and use the Extra Practice Answers page to check your answers.

Name Date

Extra Practice

Combining Sentences Using Appositive Phrases

Combining Sentences Using Appositive Phrases *(pages L183–L184)* CHAPTER 7

EXERCISE **Choose the answer in which the pair of sentences is correctly combined with an appositive.**

____ **1.** The German composer was also a pianist. The composer was Brahms.
- **A** The German composer was also a pianist; the composer was Brahms.
- **B** The German composer and pianist was Brahms.
- **C** The German composer Brahms was also a pianist.

____ **2.** Prague is the capital of the Czech Republic. It has over a million people.
- **A** Prague is the capital of the Czech Republic; it has over a million people.
- **B** The capital of the Czech Republic, Prague, has over a million people.
- **C** The capital of the Czech Republic, which has over a million people, is Prague.

____ **3.** The game is named after a sixteenth-century Italian painter. The game is Botticelli.
- **A** Botticelli is the game named after a sixteenth-century Italian painter.
- **B** The game Botticelli is named after a sixteenth-century Italian painter.
- **C** The game of Botticelli is named after a sixteenth-century Italian painter.

____ **4.** Sears and Roebuck is a large chain of retail stores in the United States. It was actually founded by Mr. Sears and Mr. Roebuck.
- **A** Sears and Roebuck is a large chain of retail stores in the United States actually founded by Mr. Sears and Mr. Roebuck.
- **B** Sears and Roebuck, a large chain of retail stores in the United States, was actually founded by Mr. Sears and Mr. Roebuck.
- **C** A large chain of retail stores in the United States called Sears and Roebuck was actually founded by Mr. Sears and Mr. Roebuck.

____ **5.** Judy Garland sang "Over the Rainbow" more than 12,000 times. It is a song from *The Wizard of Oz.*
- **A** Judy Garland sang "Over the Rainbow," a song from *The Wizard of Oz,* more than 12,000 times.
- **B** Judy Garland sang a song from *The Wizard of Oz* called "Over the Rainbow" more than 12,000 times.
- **C** Judy Garland starred in *The Wizard of Oz* and sang "Over the Rainbow" more than 12,000 times.

Name Date

Extra Practice

Identifying Phrases

Choose the answer that correctly identifies the underlined phrase in each sentence.

1. What is inside the box?
   A. adverb phrase
   B. adjective phrase
   C. misplaced modifier
   D. none of the above

2. Above the clouds, the children on the playground saw the experimental rocket.
   A. adverb phrase
   B. adjective phrase
   C. misplaced modifier
   D. none of the above

3. No, the crowd was happy instead of upset.
   A. adverb phrase
   B. adjective phrase
   C. misplaced modifier
   D. none of the above

4. Did she take the film about camels on the top shelf?
   A. adverb phrase
   B. adjective phrase
   C. misplaced modifier
   D. none of the above

5. A can of odd nuts and bolts sat beside the mechanic.
   A. adverb phrase
   B. adjective phrase
   C. misplaced modifier
   D. none of the above

Extra Practice 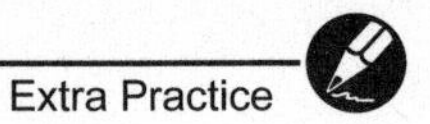

Identifying Phrases

6. A city bus lumbered slowly along the inside lane.
   A. adverb phrase
   B. adjective phrase
   C. misplaced modifier
   D. none of the above

7. Two deer in the tall bushes waited at the edge of the road.
   A. adverb phrase
   B. adjective phrase
   C. misplaced modifier
   D. none of the above

8. Learn about the past and its lessons.
   A. adverb phrase
   B. adjective phrase
   C. misplaced modifier
   D. none of the above

9. Write an essay on the Revolutionary War for next Friday.
   A. adverb phrase
   B. adjective phrase
   C. misplaced modifier
   D. none of the above

10. Ahead of us lay the Great Plains.
   A. adverb phrase
   B. adjective phrase
   C. misplaced modifier
   D. none of the above

Name Date

Extra Practice

Identifying Types of Phrases

Write the letter of the term that correctly identifies the underlined phrase in the sentence.

1. The tiny tricycle rolled slowly into my room.
   A. adjective phrase
   B. adverb phrase
   C. appositive phrase
   D. misplaced modifier

2. On the handlebars, the toddler squeezed the horn.
   A. adjective phrase
   B. adverb phrase
   C. appositive phrase
   D. misplaced modifier

3. Red streamers on the handles rustled softly.
   A. adjective phrase
   B. adverb phrase
   C. appositive phrase
   D. misplaced modifier

4. Everything was peaceful before her entrance.
   A. adjective phrase
   B. adverb phrase
   C. appositive phrase
   D. misplaced modifier

5. Actually, she shouts very quietly for a toddler.
   A. adjective phrase
   B. adverb phrase
   C. appositive phrase
   D. misplaced modifier

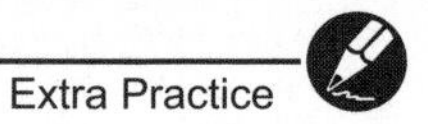

Identifying Types of Phrases

6. The toddler, my little sister Trixie, will be four on Saturday.
   A. adjective phrase
   B. adverb phrase
   C. appositive phrase
   D. misplaced modifier

7. Today, I must wrap presents for her.
   A. adjective phrase
   B. adverb phrase
   C. appositive phrase
   D. misplaced modifier

8. I bought a large, purple bear for her with a big, red nose.
   A. adjective phrase
   B. adverb phrase
   C. appositive phrase
   D. misplaced modifier

9. Mr. Ash, the shopkeeper, called it the perfect gift.
   A. adjective phrase
   B. adverb phrase
   C. appositive
   D. misplaced modifier

10. For now, how do I get her out of my room?
    A. adjective phrase
    B. adverb phrase
    C. appositive phrase
    D. misplaced modifier

Student Guide
Lesson 4: Assessment

Lesson Objectives

- Distinguish among adjective, adverb, and appositive phrases in sentences.
- Identify adjective, adverb, and appositive phrases and the words they modify or rename in sentences.
- Identify appositives and appositive phrases in sentences.
- Identify misplaced modifiers in sentences.

PREPARE

Approximate lesson time is 25 minutes.

ASSESS

Unit Checkpoint: Phrases (*Online*)

It's time to check what you have learned. Go to the next screen to test your skills.

Student Guide
Lesson 1: Participles and Participial Phrases

Have you ever tried to pat your head up and down with one hand at the same time that the other hand is making circles on your stomach? Try it; it's not as easy as it sounds. Some actions are easy to do at the same time. Other actions are hard to do at the same time.

In writing, you may need to write about two actions that are happening at the same time. Then you will probably need to use participial phrases.

Lesson Objectives

- Distinguish between participles and verbs in sentences.
- Identify participial phrases in sentences.
- Identify participles in sentences.
- Identify the words participial phrases modify in sentences.
- Identify the words participles modify in sentences.
- Recognize correct punctuation of participial phrases.

PREPARE

Approximate lesson time is 25 minutes.

Materials

For the Student

- Understanding Participles as Modifiers
- BK English Language Handbook, Level I - pages L186-L191

Optional

- Extra Practice Answers
- Finding Participles and Participial Phrases

Keywords and Pronunciation

adjective : a word that modifies, or describes, a noun or pronoun
complement : a word that helps complete the meaning of a verb
essential element : a word or a group of words that is necessary to a sentence's meaning
modifier : a word or phrase that describes or changes another word's or phrase's meaning
nonessential element : an interrupting word or group of words that is not necessary to the meaning of a sentence
participial phrase : a participle joined with related words
participle : a verb form that is used as an adjective
past participle : a verb form, often ending in -d or -ed; may be used as an adjective
present participle : the second principal part of a verb; ends in -ing and is used for all six tenses of progressive verb forms
verbal : a form of a verb that is used as another part of speech

---

LEARN

Activity 1: Participles and Participial Phrases *(Online)*

Activity 2: Participles and Participial Phrases *(Offline)*

Instructions

A. Participles

Read about participles on pages L186-L187. Then do the Understanding Participles as Modifiers page.

B. Participle or Verb?

Read about participles and verbs on page L188. Then do Check Your Understanding on pages L188-L189.

C. Participial Phrases

Read about participial phrases on pages L189-L190. Then do two Check Your Understanding exercises. Identify participial phrases and the participles within the phrases on pages L190-L191. Finally, identify the words participial phrases modify in the exercise on page L191.

D. Check Your Work

When you have finished, ask an adult to check your answers to these exercises.

E. Assessment

Go online to take the assessment.

ASSESS

Lesson Checkpoint: Participles and Participial Phrases (*Online*)

It's time to check what you have learned. Go to the next screen to test your skills.

LEARN

Activity 3. Optional: Participles and Participial Phrases *(Online)*

Name Date 

Understanding Participles as Modifiers

Underline each participle that is used as an adjective. Then draw two lines under the word it modifies.

1. Twinkling stars danced above us.
2. A bowl of steaming soup would certainly taste good.
3. His goal in life is an accounting degree.
4. Telegrams arrived for the winning candidate.
5. What is a tuning fork anyway?
6. Cindy had prepared baked chicken for dinner.
7. Submit your document in written form.
8. Have you practiced the revised lines?
9. Gradually, the frozen tundra thawed.
10. Now, blow out the lit candles!

Name Date

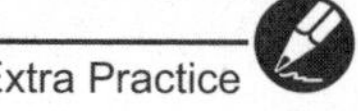

Finding Participles and Participial Phrases

Finding Participles and Participial Phrases *(pages L186–L190)*

EXERCISE **Choose the participle or participial phrase modifying the underlined noun or pronoun in each sentence.**

____ **1.** Mr. Jones spoke to the waiting <u>students.</u>
A Mr. Jones
B spoke
C to the waiting
D waiting

____ **2.** He will speak to the <u>students</u> waiting outside.
A He
B will speak
C waiting outside
D outside

____ **3.** The <u>students</u>, waiting for a test, sit quietly.
A students
B waiting
C waiting for a test
D quietly

____ **4.** Their planned <u>trip</u> to Maine begins tomorrow.
A Their
B planned
C Maine
D tomorrow

____ **5.** Planned by Mrs. Harris, the <u>trip</u> was a success.
A Planned by Mrs. Harris
B Mrs. Harris
C was
D a success

____ **6.** We must cancel the <u>trip</u> planned for today.
A We
B must cancel
C planned for today
D today

____ **7.** The <u>girl</u> waving at us is my cousin.
A waving at us
B at us
C my
D cousin

____ **8.** On the way you will pass a <u>house</u> painted yellow.
A On the way
B pass
C painted yellow
D yellow

____ **9.** <u>Grant</u>, blinded by the sun, missed the ball.
A blinded by the sun
B sun
C missed the ball
D ball

____ **10.** Walking to school, <u>Daisy</u> planned her afternoon activities.
A Walking to school
B school
C planned her afternoon activities
D activities

____ **11.** No one answered the ringing <u>doorbell</u>.
A answered
B ringing
C No one answered
D answered the ringing

____ **12.** <u>James Zaharee</u>, using a fine pen and a microscope, printed the Gettysburg Address on a human hair.
A using
B printed
C using a fine pen and a microscope
D printed the Gettysburg Address

Student Guide
Lesson 2: Gerunds

Imagine your shelf of videotapes or DVDs. When you think of a movie there, do you picture the tape itself or the title of the movie, or do you recall scenes from the film? Perhaps you move easily among all three. Part of the wonder of the human mind and of language itself is that a whole series of events can be expressed in just one word.

Very often that one word is a verbal known as a gerund.

Lesson Objectives

- Distinguish between gerunds and participles in sentences.
- Identify gerunds in sentences.
- Identify the use of gerunds in a sentence.

PREPARE

Approximate lesson time is 25 minutes.

Materials

For the Student

BK English Language Handbook, Level I - pages L193-L195

Optional

Extra Practice Answers

Identifying and Writing Gerunds

Keywords and Pronunciation

adjective : a word that modifies, or describes, a noun or pronoun

adverb : a word that modifies a verb, an adjective, or another adverb

appositive : a noun or pronoun that identifies or explains another noun or pronoun in the sentence

complement : a word that helps complete the meaning of a verb

direct object : a noun or pronoun that answers the question *What?* or *Whom?* after an action verb

gerund : a verb form ending in -ing that is used as a noun

indirect object : a noun or pronoun that answers the question *To or for whom?* or *To or for what?* after an action verb

noun : a word that names a person, place, thing, or idea

object of a preposition : a noun or pronoun that follows a preposition and completes its meaning

predicate nominative : a noun or pronoun that follows a linking verb and identifies, renames, or explains the subject

prepositional phrase : a group of words that begins with a preposition, ends with a noun or pronoun, and is used as an adjective or adverb

present participle : a verb form ending in -ing; may be used as an adjective

subject : a noun or pronoun that names whom or what a sentence is about

LEARN

Activity 1: Gerunds *(Offline)*

Instructions

A. Gerunds

Read about gerunds on page L193. Then do Check Your Understanding on pages L193-L194.

B. Gerund or Participle?

On page L194, read about distinguishing between gerunds and participles. Then do Check Your Understanding on pages L194-L195. Next, do Connect to the Writing Process on page L195.

C. Check Your Work

When you have finished, ask an adult to check your answers to these exercises.

D. Assessment

Go online to take the assessment.

ASSESS

Lesson Checkpoint: Gerunds (*Online*)

It's time to check what you have learned. Go to the next screen to test your skills.

LEARN

Activity 2. Optional: Gerunds *(Online)*

Name ____________________ Date ____________________

Extra Practice

Identifying and Writing Gerunds

A. Identifying Gerunds

Underline the gerund in each of the following sentences.

1. Fishing is a popular sport around here.
2. People take casting quite seriously and train their children at an early age.
3. As for me, I prefer crabbing.
4. To my sister, the most distasteful task has always been the cleaning.
5. What is the best fish for baking?

B. Writing Gerunds

For each sentence, write an appropriate gerund in the blank.

6. My favorite sport is __________.
7. __________ makes me happy.
8. I have always dreamed of one day __________.
9. On the other hand, I dislike __________.
10. Learn __________, and you will never regret it.

Student Guide
Lesson 3: Gerund Phrases

Think back. What were your favorite activities when you were five years old? Coloring with crayons? Blowing bubbles? Perhaps playing hide and seek was more your style.

Whatever you answer, you'll probably use a gerund phrase to describe it. Gerund phrases may be the most economical way of expressing an action.

Lesson Objectives

- Identify gerund phrases in sentences.
- Identify the use of gerund phrases in sentences.

PREPARE

Approximate lesson time is 25 minutes.

Materials

For the Student

BK English Language Handbook, Level I - pages L195-L197

Optional

Extra Practice Answers

Finding Gerunds and Gerund Phrases

Keywords and Pronunciation

adjective : a word that modifies, or describes, a noun or pronoun
adverb : a word that modifies a verb, an adjective, or another adverb
appositive : a noun or pronoun that identifies or explains another noun or pronoun in the sentence
complement : a word that helps complete the meaning of a verb
direct object : a noun or pronoun that answers the question *What?* or *Whom?* after an action verb
gerund phrase : a gerund with its modifiers and complements--all working together as a noun
indirect object : a noun or pronoun that answers the question *To or for whom?* or *To or for what?* after an action verb
modifier : a word or phrase that describes or changes another word's or phrase's meaning
noun : a word that names a person, place, thing, or idea
object of a preposition : a noun or pronoun that follows a preposition and completes its meaning
predicate nominative : a noun or pronoun that follows a linking verb and identifies, renames, or explains the subject
prepositional phrase : a group of words that begins with a preposition, ends with a noun or pronoun, and is used as an adjective or adverb

LEARN

Activity 1: Gerund Phrases *(Offline)*

Instructions

A. Gerund Phrases

Read about gerund phrases on pages L195-L197. Then do two exercises. First do Check Your Understanding on page L196. Then do Check Your Understanding on the next page, L197.

B. Check Your Work

When you have finished, ask an adult to check your answers to these exercises.

C. Assessment

Go online to take the assessment.

ASSESS

Lesson Checkpoint: Gerund phrases (*Online*)

It's time to check what you have learned. Go to the next screen to test your skills.

LEARN

Activity 2. Optional: Gerund Phrases *(Online)*

Name Date

Extra Practice

Finding Gerunds and Gerund Phrases

Finding Gerunds and Gerund Phrases

(pages L193–L196) **CHAPTER 7**

EXERCISE **Choose the complete gerund or gerund phrase in each sentence.**

____ **1.** Cheering the team gave me a sore throat.
A Cheering
B Cheering the team
C gave me
D a sore throat

____ **2.** My uncle is taking up a new kind of exercise, walking.
A My uncle
B taking
C taking up a new kind of exercise
D walking

____ **3.** Juana's mother enjoys preserving fruits and vegetables.
A Juana's mother
B enjoys
C preserving fruits
D preserving fruits and vegetables

____ **4.** Coming early was the right thing to do.
A Coming
B Coming early
C the right thing
D to do

____ **5.** The puppy's soft whining was coming from under the stairs.
A The puppy's soft whining
B whining
C was coming from
D under the stairs

____ **6.** Swimming is one of the best forms of exercise.
A Swimming
B best
C exercise
D best

____ **7.** Galileo made his first telescope by placing a lens at each end of an organ pipe.
A made his first telescope
B placing
C placing a lens at each end of an organ pipe
D telescope

____ **8.** She has just finished a course in typing.
A course
B She
C course in typing
D typing

____ **9.** Please stop that yelling!
A yelling
B that yelling
C Please
D stop that

____ **10.** Sinking 499 free throws in a row is Ellen's present claim to fame.
A claim
B Sinking 499 free throws in a row
C claim to fame
D Sinking

____ **11.** An early method of food preservation was pickling.
A pickling
B preservation
C method
D food

____ **12.** A snail can cross the edge of the sharpest razor without cutting itself.
A cutting
B cutting itself
C cross
D edge of the sharpest razor

Student Guide
Lesson 4: Infinitives and Infinitive Phrases

"You have great potential, kid!" Has anyone ever said those words to you? They mean that you have abilities that give you possibilities in the future--to excel, to achieve, to be something or somebody special.

These words, *to excel, to achieve,* and *to be,* are the infinitive form of a verb. Infinitives and infinitive phrases are the third kind of verbal.

Lesson Objectives

- Distinguish between infinitives and prepositional phrases in sentences.
- Identify infinitives and infinitive phrases in sentences.
- Identify the use of infinitives and infinitive phrases in sentences.

PREPARE

Approximate lesson time is 25 minutes.

Materials

For the Student

BK English Language Handbook, Level I - pages L198-L203

Optional

- Distinguishing Between Infinitives and Preposition
- Extra Practice Answers
- Using Infinitives and Infinitive Phrases

Keywords and Pronunciation

adjective : a word that modifies, or describes, a noun or pronoun

adverb : a word that modifies a verb, an adjective, or another adverb

infinitive : the verb form that usually begins with to*;* used as a noun, adjective, or adverb

infinitive phrase : an infinitive with its modifiers and complements, working together as a noun, adjective, or adverb

noun : a word that names a person, place, thing, or idea

prepositional phrase : a group of words that begins with a preposition, ends with a noun or pronoun, and is used as an adjective or adverb

verb : a word used to express an action or a state of being

LEARN

Activity 1: Infinitives and Infinitive Phrases *(Offline)*

Instructions

A. Infinitives

Read about infinitives on pages L198-L199. Then do Check Your Understanding on page L199.

B. Infinitive or Prepositional Phrase?

Read about infinitives and prepositional phrases on pages L199-L200. Then do Check Your Understanding on page L200.

C. Infinitive Phrases

Read about infinitive phrases on pages L201-L202. Then do items 1-5 of Check Your Understanding on page L202, and items 11-20 of Check Your Understanding on page L203.

D. Check Your Work

When you have finished, ask an adult to check your answers to these exercises.

E. Assessment

Go online to take the assessment.

ASSESS

Lesson Assessment: Infinitives and Infinitive Phrases (*Online*)

It's time to check what you have learned. Go to the next screen to test your skills.

LEARN

Activity 2. Optional: Infinitives and Infinitive Phrases *(Online)*

Name Date

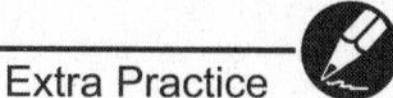
Extra Practice

Distinguishing Between Infinitives and Prepositional Phrases

___ **1.** Han hurried to dress.
A infinitive
B prepositional phrase

___ **2.** He hurried to school.
A infinitive
B prepositional phrase

___ **3.** His class was going to the mint.
A infinitive
B prepositional phrase

___ **4.** He needed to arrive early.
A infinitive
B prepositional phrase

___ **5.** He wanted to stop at the library.
A infinitive
B prepositional phrase

___ **6.** He went there to return a book.
A infinitive
B prepositional phrase

___ **7.** He handed it to the librarian.
A infinitive
B prepositional phrase

___ **8.** He had read it to learn about coins.
A infinitive
B prepositional phrase

___ **9.** He planned to write a report about money.
A infinitive
B prepositional phrase

___ **10.** To visit the mint would be useful.
A infinitive
B prepositional phrase

Name Date

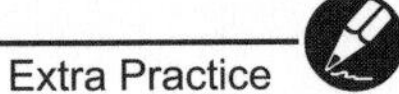

Extra Practice

Using Infinitives and Infinitive Phrases

Identify how each underlined phrase is used in the sentence.

1. Do you know the name of the person to see?

   A. infinitive used as a noun
   B. infinitive used as an adjective
   C. infinitive used as an adverb
   D. prepositional phrase

2. Now I would like to speak.

   A. infinitive used as a noun
   B. infinitive used as an adjective
   C. infinitive used as an adverb
   D. prepositional phrase

3. Should we take the dog to Tennessee with us?

   A. infinitive used as a noun
   B. infinitive used as an adjective
   C. infinitive used as an adverb
   D. prepositional phrase

4. Jeff just learned to ski.

   A. infinitive used as a noun
   B. infinitive used as an adjective
   C. infinitive used as an adverb
   D. prepositional phrase

5. That computer is too expensive to buy.

   A. infinitive used as a noun
   B. infinitive used as an adjective
   C. infinitive used as an adverb
   D. prepositional phrase

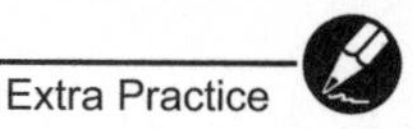

Using Infinitives and Infinitive Phrases

6. What do you want to say?

   A. infinitive used as a noun
   B. infinitive used as an adjective
   C. infinitive used as an adverb
   D. prepositional phrase

7. The movie to see this summer is showing at the Plaza.

   A. infinitive phrase used as a noun
   B. infinitive phrase used as an adjective
   C. infinitive phrase used as an adverb
   D. prepositional phrase

8. The oboe is hard to master.

   A. infinitive used as a noun
   B. infinitive used as an adjective
   C. infinitive used as an adverb
   D. prepositional phrase

9. The best way to go to Jackie's house is Route 62.

   A. infinitive phrase used as a noun
   B. infinitive phrase used as an adjective
   C. infinitive phrase used as an adverb
   D. prepositional phrase

10. To write well, think well.

   A. infinitive phrase used as a noun
   B. infinitive phrase used as an adjective
   C. infinitive phrase used as an adverb
   D. prepositional phrase

Student Guide
Lesson 5: Misplaced and Dangling Modifiers

Imagine this: The mayor of your city is going to give you an award at a special banquet. You arrive dressed in all new finery. There you are, wearing your new shoes as you walk in, when suddenly disaster strikes. You trip and fall flat on your face, smashing into a table and knocking a glass of water right in the mayor's lap!
Whether it's a misplaced foot or a misplaced modifier, you can avoid embarrassment by watching your step.

Lesson Objectives

- Distinguish between correctly placed and misplaced or dangling modifiers.
- Revise sentences to correct misplaced or dangling modifiers.

PREPARE

Approximate lesson time is 25 minutes.

Materials

For the Student

BK English Language Handbook, Level I - pages L204-L206

Optional

Extra Practice Answers

Finding the Words Modified by Misplaced Modifiers

Keywords and Pronunciation

dangling modifier : a verbal phrase that does not modify any word or group of words in a sentence
infinitive phrase : an infinitive with its modifiers and complements, working together as a noun, adjective, or adverb
misplaced modifier : a word or phrase that seems to modify the wrong word or words because it is too far from what it describes
noun : a word that names a person, place, thing, or idea
participial phrase : a participle joined with related words
pronoun : a word that takes the place of one or more nouns
verbal phrase : a verb along with its modifiers

LEARN

Activity 1: Misplaced and Dangling Modifiers *(Offline)*

Instructions

A. Misplaced and Dangling Modifiers

Read about misplaced and dangling modifiers on pages L204-L205. Then do Check Your Understanding on pages L205-L206 and Connect to the Writing Process, also on page L206.

B. Check Your Work

When you have finished, ask an adult to check your answers to these exercises.

C. Assessment

Go online to take the assessment.

ASSESS

Lesson Checkpoint: Misplaced and Dangling Modifiers (*Online*)

It's time to check what you have learned. Go to the next screen to test your skills.

LEARN

Activity 2. Optional: Misplaced and Dangling Modifiers *(Online)*

Name ______________________ Date ______________________

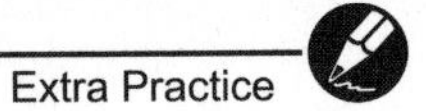

Finding the Words Modified by Misplaced Modifiers

Choose the correct noun or pronoun that each underlined misplaced modifier should modify.

____ **1.** Ramon saw an airplane walking home.
A Ramon
B airplane

____ **2.** Mrs. Smith left the house covered in fur.
A Mrs. Smith
B house

____ **3.** Cleaning her feathers, Marvella saw a duck.
A Marvella
B duck

____ **4.** A man gave some bread to the pigeon carrying a suitcase.
A man
B pigeon

____ **5.** Patrick built a house for the dog made of wood.
A house
B dog

____ **6.** The bird-watcher spotted a heron using high-powered binoculars.
A bird-watcher
B heron

____ **7.** Tom swatted the mosquito muttering quietly.
A Tom
B mosquito

____ **8.** Falling to the ground, Amy's eyes followed the shooting star.
A eyes
B star

____ **9.** We finally saw the exhibit in the museum praised by everyone.
A exhibit
B museum

____ **10.** The actress rehearsed her part in the theater showing great emotion.
A actress
B theater

____ **11.** Jack noticed two robins bicycling to school.
A Jack
B robins

____ **12.** I came upon an accident turning the corner.
A accident
B I

____ **13.** Covered in whipped cream, I ate the delicious strawberries.
A I
B strawberries

____ **14.** That gift was given by Eric wrapped in silver paper.
A That
B gift

____ **15.** Described in detail, I imagined the images in the book.
A images
B book

____ **16.** We noticed a stranger at the front door looking out the upstairs window.
A We
B stranger

Student Guide
Lesson 6: Review

In this lesson, you will answer some review questions on what you learned in this unit about verbals and verbal phrases and misplaced and dangling modifiers. Before you take the Unit Assessment, this is your chance to find out what you do and don't know about identifying verbals and verbal phrases, such as participial phrases, gerund phrases, and infinitive phrases, as well as identifying how verbal phrases are used in sentences.

Lesson Objectives

- Distinguish among the three kinds of verbals and verbal phrases.
- Distinguish between correctly placed and misplaced or dangling modifiers.
- Identify gerunds and gerund phrases in sentences.
- Identify infinitives and infinitive phrases in sentences.
- Identify participles and participial phrases in sentences.
- Identify the use of gerunds and gerund phrases in sentences.
- Identify the use of infinitives and infinitive phrases in sentences.
- Identify the words participles and participial phrases modify in sentences.

PREPARE

Approximate lesson time is 25 minutes.

Materials

For the Student

BK English Language Handbook, Level I - pages L210-L211, L206-L207, L212-L213

Optional

Extra Practice Answers

BK English Language Handbook, Level I - pages L216-L217

Keywords and Pronunciation

adjective : a word that modifies, or describes, a noun or pronoun
adverb : a word that modifies a verb, an adjective, or another adverb
appositive : a noun or pronoun that identifies or explains another noun or pronoun in the sentence
complement : a word that helps complete the meaning of a verb
dangling modifier : a verbal phrase that does not modify any word or group of words in a sentence
direct object : a noun or pronoun that answers the question *What?* or *Whom?* after an action verb
essential element : a word or a group of words that is necessary to a sentence's meaning
gerund : a verb form ending in -ing that is used as a noun
gerund phrase : a gerund with its modifiers and complements--all working together as a noun
indirect object : a noun or pronoun that answers the question *To or for whom?* or *To or for what?* after an action verb
infinitive : the verb form that usually begins with to*;* used as a noun, adjective, or adverb

infinitive phrase : an infinitive with its modifiers and complements, working together as a noun, adjective, or adverb
misplaced modifier : a word or phrase that seems to modify the wrong word or words because it is too far from what it describes
modifier : a word or phrase that describes or changes another word's or phrase's meaning
nonessential element : an interrupting word or group of words that is not necessary to the meaning of a sentence
noun : a word that names a person, place, thing, or idea
object of a preposition : a noun or pronoun that follows a preposition and completes its meaning
participial phrase : a participle joined with related words
participle : a verb form that is used as an adjective
past participle : a verb form, often ending in -d or -ed; may be used as an adjective
predicate nominative : a noun or pronoun that follows a linking verb and identifies, renames, or explains the subject
prepositional phrase : a group of words that begins with a preposition, ends with a noun or pronoun, and is used as an adjective or adverb
present participle : a verb form ending in -ing; may be used as an adjective
pronoun : a word that takes the place of one or more nouns
subject : a noun or pronoun that names whom or what a sentence is about
verb : a word used to express an action or a state of being
verbal : a form of a verb that is used as another part of speech
verbal phrase : a verb along with its modifiers

LEARN

Activity 1: Verbals and Verbal Phrases *(Offline)*

Instructions

A. Review

To prepare for the Unit Assessment, read pages L210-L211 about diagraming verbal phrases and then diagram the sentences in Practice Your Skills on page L211. Next do QuickCheck on pages L206-L207. Then complete Identifying Verbal Phrases in the CheckPoint exercise on pages L212-L213.

B. Check Your Work

When you have finished, have an adult check your answers. Make sure you understand the corrections for any mistakes you made. If you do that, then you should be ready for the Unit Assessment.

Activity 2. Optional: Verbals and Verbal Phrases *(Offline)*

Instructions

Extra Practice: Complete the Posttest exercise on pages L216-L217.

When you have finished, use the Extra Practice Answers page to check your answers.

Student Guide
Lesson 7: Assessment

Lesson Objectives

- Distinguish among the three kinds of verbals and verbal phrases.
- Distinguish between correctly placed and misplaced or dangling modifiers.
- Identify gerunds and gerund phrases in sentences.
- Identify infinitives and infinitive phrases in sentences.
- Identify participles and participial phrases in sentences.
- Identify the use of gerunds and gerund phrases in sentences.
- Identify the use of infinitives and infinitive phrases in sentences.
- Identify the words participles and participial phrases modify in sentences.

PREPARE

Approximate lesson time is 25 minutes.

ASSESS

Unit Checkpoint: Verbals and Verbal Phrases (*Online*)

It's time to check what you have learned. Go to the next screen to test your skills.

Student Guide
Lesson 1: Independent and Subordinate Clauses

Have you ever heard the term *shipshape*? It's a navy term that means "perfect order." In the navy, everything must be in perfect order, including people. You can identify the rank of anyone by his or her hat, rank insignia, or stripes. These signs make it easy to tell the ranking officer who gives orders from the subordinate officer who takes orders.

There are signs that make it easy to recognize independent clauses and subordinate clauses. If you learn the signs, then identifying clauses is easy.

Lesson Objectives

- Distinguish between independent and subordinate clauses in sentences.

PREPARE

Approximate lesson time is 25 minutes.

Materials

For the Student

BK English Language Handbook, Level I - pages L221-L223

Optional

Extra Practice Answers

Independent and Subordinate Clauses

Keywords and Pronunciation

adjective : a word that modifies, or describes, a noun or pronoun

adverb : a word that modifies a verb, an adjective, or another adverb

antecedent (an-tuh-SEE-duhnt) : a word or group of words that a pronoun replaces, or refers to

clause : a group of words that has a subject and a verb

dependent clause : another name for a subordinate clause

independent, or main, clause : a clause that can stand alone as a sentence because it expresses a complete idea

main clause : another name for an independent clause

modifier : a word or phrase that describes or changes another word's or phrase's meaning

noun : a word that names a person, place, thing, or idea

noun clause : a subordinate clause that is used as a noun

phrase : a group of related words that acts as a single part of speech

relative pronoun : a pronoun that relates an adjective clause to the noun or pronoun the clause describes

sentence : a group of words that contains a subject and a verb and expresses a complete thought

simple sentence : a sentence that has one subject and one verb, either or both of which may be compound

subject : a noun or pronoun that names whom or what a sentence is about

subordinate, or dependent, clause : a clause that cannot stand alone as a sentence because it does not express a complete thought

verb : a word used to express an action or a state of being

LEARN

Activity 1: Independent and Subordinate Clauses *(Online)*

Activity 2: Independent and Subordinate Clauses *(Offline)*

Instructions

A. Independent and Subordinate Clauses

Read about independent and subordinate clauses on pages L221-L222. Then do Check Your Understanding on page L223.

B. Check Your Work

When you have finished, ask an adult to check your answers to this exercise.

C. Assessment

Go online to take the assessment.

ASSESS

Lesson Checkpoint: Independent and Subordinate Clauses (*Online*)

It's time to check what you have learned. Go to the next screen to test your skills.

LEARN

Activity 3. Optional: Independent and Subordinate Clauses *(Online)*

Name Date

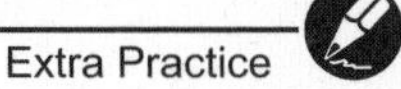
Extra Practice

Independent and Subordinate Clauses

Identify each underlined clause as either an independent or a subordinate clause by writing the letter *I* or *S* next to each sentence.

1. Mrs. Santos sat in the chair.
2. Mrs. Santos sat in the chair, and Maggie sat on the floor.
3. Mrs. Santos sat in the chair as she talked to Maggie.
4. The telephone rang.
5. If the telephone rings, Luke will answer it.
6. When the telephone rang, Luke had already left the house.
7. While he was out, the answering machine picked up the call.
8. Take a message unless the machine has been turned on.
9. The message was useless because the note had been lost.
10. Tell me what I should do about this problem.
11. Do you know where I can buy a better machine?
12. Although their machine is old, it works well.
13. As long as I have this problem, I will miss calls.
14. Since I missed your call, I am determined to solve this problem.
15. Actually, the solution was easier than I had thought.

Student Guide
Lesson 2: Adverb Clauses

Wouldn't you like to hear someone say to you, "I'll give you a million dollars"? But you know that is very unlikely. And if someone were to say it, there would be conditions, such as, "if you can swim the Atlantic" or "when you win the Olympics" or even "as soon as you can be quiet for just one day." It's those little words like *if*, *when*, and *as soon as* that make all the difference!
Those are the same words that will help you identify subordinate clauses, especially adverb clauses.

Lesson Objectives

- Identify adverb clauses in sentences.
- Identify the word the adverb clause modifies.
- Recognize the correct punctuation of sentences with adverb clauses.
- Recognize the correct punctuation of sentences with adjective clauses.

PREPARE

Approximate lesson time is 25 minutes.

Materials

For the Student

BK English Language Handbook, Level I - pages L224-L227

Optional

Adverb Clauses

Extra Practice Answers

Keywords and Pronunciation

adjective : a word that modifies, or describes, a noun or pronoun
adverb : a word that modifies a verb, an adjective, or another adverb
adverb clause : a subordinate clause that is used mainly to modify a verb
adverb phrase : a prepositional phrase that is used to modify a verb, adjective, or adverb
noun : a word that names a person, place, thing, or idea
preposition : a word that shows the relationship between a noun or a pronoun and another word in the sentence
subordinate, or dependent, clause : a clause that cannot stand alone as a sentence because it does not express a complete thought
subordinating conjunction : a conjunction that introduces an adverb clause
verb : a word used to express an action or a state of being

LEARN

Activity 1: Adverb Clauses *(Offline)*

Instructions

A. Adverb Clauses, Subordinating Conjunctions, and Punctuation

Read about adverb clauses, subordinating conjunctions, and punctuation with adverb clauses on pages L224-L226. Then do two Check Your Understanding exercises; the first is on page L226, and the second exercise begins on that same page and continues on page L227. Next do items 21-24 of Connect to the Writing Process.

> **Note** – Omit #25 on page L227 because there is no adverb clause in the sentence.

B. Check Your Work

When you have finished, ask an adult to check your answers to these exercises.

C. Assessment

Go online to take the assessment.

ASSESS

Lesson Checkpoint: Adverb Clauses (*Online*)

It's time to check what you have learned. Go to the next screen to test your skills.

LEARN

Activity 2. Optional: Adverb Clauses *(Online)*

Name Date

Extra Practice 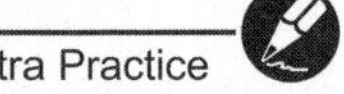

Adverb Clauses

CHAPTER 8 Adverb Clauses *(pages L224–L226)*

EXERCISE A **Choose the complete adverb clause in each sentence.**

____ **1.** When the curtain falls, the audience applauds.
A When the curtain falls
B the audience applauds

____ **2.** If the telephone rings, Paul will answer it.
A If the telephone rings
B Paul will answer it

____ **3.** That dish has been cracked since Lillian dropped it.
A That dish has been cracked
B since Lillian dropped it

____ **4.** Wilbur listened to the radio while he folded the laundry.
A to the radio
B while he folded the laundry

____ **5.** The dress will fit Becky as long as she doesn't grow.
A will fit Becky
B as long as she doesn't grow

____ **6.** Before clocks were invented, various devices were used to tell time.
A Before clocks were invented
B used to tell time

____ **7.** Sundials were effective as long as the sun was shining.
A were effective
B as long as the sun was shining

____ **8.** Ropes tied in regularly spaced knots measured time as they burned.
A in regularly spaced knots
B as they burned

____ **9.** When all the sand had trickled through the narrow midsection of an hourglass, an hour had passed.
A When all the sand had trickled through the narrow midsection of an hourglass
B of an hourglass

____ **10.** Convenient and accurate timekeeping did not exist until clocks came into use in the 1700s.
A Convenient and accurate
B until clocks came into use in the 1700s

____ **11.** United States Marines are called leathernecks because their coats once had big leather collars.
A are called leathernecks
B because their coats once had big leather collars

____ **12.** A tornado once sheared a whole herd of sheep while they grazed.
A once sheared
B while they grazed

____ **13.** I will exercise as long as you do.
A will exercise
B as long as you do

____ **14.** Although Columbus made four voyages to the Americas, he never discovered the coast of the mainland.
A Although Columbus made four voyages to the Americas
B never discovered the coast of the mainland

____ **15.** Unless I set the alarm, I will sleep until nine o'clock and be late for school.
A Unless I set the alarm
B be late for school

____ **16.** The quality of programs on television declines when summer comes.
A quality of programs on television
B when summer comes

Student Guide
Lesson 3: Adjective Clauses

Have you ever had two or more friends who have the same name? How confusing that situation can be! You'll end up saying things like, "I mean the Tim that lives next door" or "Not *that* Mr. Fox, but the Mr. Fox whose daughter is on our team."

To clear up the matter of who's who, you need adjective clauses.

Lesson Objectives

- Identify adjective clauses in sentences.
- Identify the word the adjective clause modifies.

PREPARE

Approximate lesson time is 25 minutes.

Materials

For the Student

BK English Language Handbook, Level I - pages L229-L231

Optional

Adjective Clauses and Relative Pronouns

Extra Practice Answers

Keywords and Pronunciation

adjective clause : a subordinate clause that is used to modify a noun or pronoun
adjective phrase : a prepositional phrase that modifies a noun or pronoun
antecedent (an-tuh-SEE-duhnt) : a word or group of words that a pronoun replaces, or refers to
noun : a word that names a person, place, thing, or idea
pronoun : a word that takes the place of one or more nouns
relative pronoun : a pronoun that relates an adjective clause to the noun or pronoun the clause describes
subordinate, or dependent, clause : a clause that cannot stand alone as a sentence because it does not express a complete thought

LEARN

Activity 1: Adjective Clauses *(Offline)*

Instructions

A. Adjective Clauses, Relative Pronouns

Read about adjective clauses and relative pronouns on pages L229-L230. Then do items 1-5 of the Check Your Understanding exercise on pages L230-L231. Next complete Check Your Understanding on page L231.

B. Check Your Work

When you have finished, ask an adult to check your answers to these exercises.

C. Assessment

Go online to take the assessment.

ASSESS

Lesson Checkpoint: Adjective Clauses (*Online*)

It's time to check what you have learned. Go to the next screen to test your skills.

LEARN

Activity 2. Optional: Adjective Clauses *(Online)*

Name ______________________ Date ______________________

Extra Practice

Adjective Clauses and Relative Pronouns – Part A

CHAPTER 8 Adjective Clauses and Relative Pronouns *(pages L229–L234)*

EXERCISE A Choose the adjective clause in each sentence.

____ **1.** My mother and I are going to the sale that the antique store is having.
A to the sale
B that the antique store is having

____ **2.** This is the catalog which came in the mail last week.
A This is the catalog
B which came in the mail last week

____ **3.** The numbers that are written in red show the sale prices.
A that are written in red
B show the sale prices

____ **4.** Mrs. Harper, who lives next door, will come with us.
A who lives next door
B with us

____ **5.** That chair is the piece of furniture that she wants.
A That chair
B that she wants

____ **6.** Unlike the organ, which dates back to Roman times, the piano is fairly modern.
A Unlike the organ
B which dates back to Roman times

____ **7.** Cristofori, who built the first piano, lived in Italy in the early eighteenth century.
A who built the first piano
B lived in Italy

____ **8.** Then German craftsmen, for whom every musical instrument was a challenge, improved its design.
A for whom every musical instrument was a challenge
B its design

____ **9.** By the 1770s, the piano had become the instrument that every European wanted.
A By the 1770s
B that every European wanted

____ **10.** It was the rare upper-class family whose household did not include a piano.
A whose household did not include a piano
B include a piano

Student Guide
Lesson 4: Functions of Relative Pronouns

Once upon a time, there were no street signs. However, people didn't have too much trouble getting around. Towns were small, so finding a particular place was not difficult. Besides, everyone knew one another. In today's world, we need street signs. In fact, we need lots of different kinds of signs: stop signs, yield signs, deer crossing signs, and curves ahead signs.

Relative pronouns are like street signs. These special pronouns tell you that an adjective clause is probably coming right up.

Lesson Objectives

- Identify the function of a relative pronoun in a sentence.
- Recognize misplaced adjective clauses in sentences.
- Recognize the correct punctuation of sentences with adjective clauses.

PREPARE

Approximate lesson time is 25 minutes.

Materials

For the Student

BK English Language Handbook, Level I - pages L232-L237

Optional

- Adjective Clauses and Relative Pronouns
- Extra Practice Answers
- Misplaced Modifiers

Keywords and Pronunciation

adjective clause : a subordinate clause that is used to modify a noun or pronoun
direct object : a noun or pronoun that answers the question *What?* or *Whom?* after an action verb
essential clause : a clause that is necessary to a sentence's meaning
misplaced modifier : a word or phrase that seems to modify the wrong word or words because it is too far from what it describes
modifier : a word or phrase that describes or changes another word's or phrase's meaning
nonessential clause : a clause that is not necessary to a sentence's meaning
object of a preposition : a noun or pronoun that follows a preposition and completes its meaning
relative pronoun : a pronoun that relates an adjective clause to the noun or pronoun the clause describes
subject : a noun or pronoun that names whom or what a sentence is about

LEARN

Activity 1: Functions of Relative Pronouns *(Offline)*

Instructions

A. Functions of Relative Pronouns

Read about relative pronouns on pages L232-L233. Then do Check Your Understanding on pages L233-L234.

B. Misplaced Modifiers

Read about misplaced modifiers on pages L235-L236. Then do Check Your Understanding on page L236 and Connect to the Writing Process on page L237.

C. Check Your Work

When you have finished, ask an adult to check your answers to these exercises.

D. Assessment

Go online to take the assessment.

ASSESS

Lesson Checkpoint: Functions of Relative Pronouns (*Online*)

It's time to check what you have learned. Go to the next screen to test your skills.

LEARN

Activity 2. Optional: Functions of Relative Pronouns *(Online)*

Name ______________________ Date ______________________

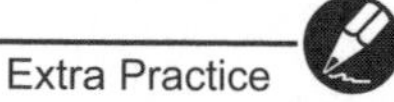

Adjective Clauses and Relative Pronouns – Part B

Adjective Clauses and Relative Pronouns *(pages L229–L234)*

EXERCISE B **Decide the function of each relative pronoun (some are understood) in the underlined adjective clause in each sentence.**

____ **1.** The Carters, whose dog I walk, will be away for three weeks.
A subject
B direct object
C object of a preposition
D possessive

____ **2.** Lions that are raised in captivity are surprisingly tame.
A subject
B direct object
C object of a preposition
D possessive

____ **3.** Are you wearing the coat you bought last week at the mall?
A subject
B direct object
C object of a preposition
D possessive

____ **4.** The longest tunnel through which we drove was about a mile long.
A subject
B direct object
C object of a preposition
D possessive

____ **5.** Daniel Webster, who became famous for his work in law, never went to law school.
A subject
B direct object
C object of a preposition
D possessive

____ **6.** The records I gave him dated back to the 1950s.
A subject
B direct object
C object of a preposition
D possessive

____ **7.** The story, whose author was unknown, was comical.
A subject
B direct object
C object of a preposition
D possessive

____ **8.** A rat can gnaw through concrete that is two feet thick.
A subject
B direct object
C object of a preposition
D possessive

____ **9.** He is the man to whom you must speak.
A subject
B direct object
C object of a preposition
D possessive

____ **10.** The ostrich, which is the largest of all birds, can outrun a horse.
A subject
B direct object
C object of a preposition
D possessive

Name ____________________ Date ____________________

Extra Practice 

Misplaced Modifiers

Misplaced Modifiers *(pages L235–L236)*

EXERCISE A **Choose the word that the misplaced modifier should modify.**

____ **1.** The birds ignored the dog that chirped in the trees.
- **A** dog
- **B** trees
- **C** that
- **D** birds

____ **2.** The present is on the table that I received for my birthday.
- **A** table
- **B** present
- **C** I
- **D** birthday

____ **3.** The ten-speed bicycle is in the garage that my father bought for me.
- **A** garage
- **B** father
- **C** bicycle
- **D** that

____ **4.** The movie will be shown in the auditorium which has Antarctica as the setting.
- **A** movie
- **B** Antarctica
- **C** auditorium
- **D** setting

____ **5.** Glenn repaired my car who's a good friend of mine.
- **A** Glenn
- **B** car
- **C** friend
- **D** mine

____ **6.** We met Mrs. Walker in the park who lives nearby.
- **A** park
- **B** We
- **C** Mrs. Walker
- **D** who

____ **7.** The note was a reminder to order Pat's birthday cake that was written on the calendar.
- **A** reminder
- **B** cake
- **C** calendar
- **D** note

____ **8.** The CD is in the cabinet that I thought I had lost.
- **A** cabinet
- **B** that
- **C** lost
- **D** CD

____ **9.** The rain flooded our basement which lasted a week.
- **A** week
- **B** rain
- **C** which
- **D** basement

____ **10.** The oak tree provides us with shade that grows in our backyard.
- **A** tree
- **B** that
- **C** shade
- **D** backyard

____ **11.** The teenager that Santana had released bought the most recent CD.
- **A** teenager
- **B** Santana
- **C** CD
- **D** that

____ **12.** The students did not have to take the final exam whose average was an A.
- **A** exam
- **B** A
- **C** average
- **D** students

Student Guide
Lesson 5: Noun Clauses

What today's lesson teaches may be brand new. You will learn that adjective clauses and adverb clauses are not the only kind of subordinate clauses. A third kind of subordinate clause is what you will find out about today. Can you guess what kind of clause it is?

If you guessed noun clause, you guessed correctly. In fact, there are four noun clauses in the first paragraph. Each sentence in that paragraph has one noun clause.

Lesson Objectives

- Identify noun clauses in sentences.
- Identify the use of a noun clause in a sentence.

PREPARE

Approximate lesson time is 25 minutes.

Materials

For the Student

BK English Language Handbook, Level I - pages L237-L240

Optional

Extra Practice Answers

Identifying Noun Clauses and Their Uses

Keywords and Pronunciation

adjective clause : a subordinate clause that is used to modify a noun or pronoun

adverb clause : a subordinate clause that is used mainly to modify a verb

direct object : a noun or pronoun that answers the question *What?* or *Whom?* after an action verb

indirect object : a noun or pronoun that answers the question *To or for whom?* or *To or for what?* after an action verb

noun : a word that names a person, place, thing, or idea

noun clause : a subordinate clause that is used as a noun

object of a preposition : a noun or pronoun that follows a preposition and completes its meaning

predicate nominative : a noun or pronoun that follows a linking verb and identifies, renames, or explains the subject

subject : a noun or pronoun that names whom or what a sentence is about

subordinate, or dependent, clause : a clause that cannot stand alone as a sentence because it does not express a complete thought

LEARN

Activity 1: Noun Clauses *(Offline)*

Instructions

A. Noun Clauses

Read about noun clauses on pages L237-L238. Then do Check Your Understanding on pages L238-L239. Also do the next Check Your Understanding on page L239 and Connect to the Writing Process on pages L239-L240.

B. Check Your Work

When you have finished, ask an adult to check your answers to these exercises.

C. Assessment

Go online to take the assessment.

ASSESS

Lesson Checkpoint: Noun Clauses (*Online*)

It's time to check what you have learned. Go to the next screen to test your skills.

LEARN

Activity 2. Optional: Noun Clauses *(Online)*

Name Date

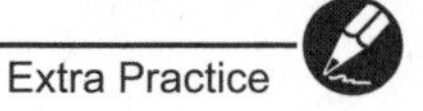
Extra Practice

Identifying Noun Clauses and Their Uses

Exercise A – Identifying Noun Clauses

Underline the noun clause in each of the following sentences.

1. We will take a vote and do whatever the majority wants.
2. That is where it's happening.
3. Are you really concerned with what is best for me?
4. Offer whoever attends the meeting a bumper sticker.
5. What you say is true up to a point.
6. Steve was unclear about when we were leaving.
7. I don't know what you mean.
8. The award will go to whomever the committee chooses.
9. That trees require huge quantities of water does not surprise me.
10. The eruptions of volcanoes are what Dr. Sweeney is studying.

Exercise B – Identifying the Uses of Noun Clauses

Label each noun clause in the above sentences. Write *subject, direct object, indirect object, object of a preposition,* or *predicate nominative.*

Student Guide
Lesson 6: Sentence Structure

If you had two red blocks and one green block, how many different combinations could you make if every combination included at least one red block? Do you remember solving puzzles like this one when you were younger? At first, they seemed difficult; then you realized how easy they really were.

Like learning to solve puzzles, understanding sentence structure should become easy with practice.

Lesson Objectives

- Identify sentences as simple, compound, complex, or compound-complex.
- Recognize correctly punctuated compound sentences.

PREPARE

Approximate lesson time is 25 minutes.

Materials

For the Student

BK English Language Handbook, Level I - pages L242-L245

Optional

Extra Practice Answers

Sentence Structure

Keywords and Pronunciation

complex sentence : a sentence that consists of one independent clause and one or more subordinate clauses
compound sentence : two or more simple sentences, joined by a comma and coordinating conjunction or by a semicolon
compound subject : two or more subjects connected by *and* or *or* that have the same verb
compound verb : two or more verbs connected by *and* or *or* that have the same subject
compound-complex sentence : a sentence that consists of two or more independent clauses and at least one subordinate clause
independent, or main, clause : a clause that can stand alone as a sentence because it expresses a complete idea
sentence structure : the combination of independent and subordinate clauses in a sentence; the four different kinds of sentence structure are simple, compound, complex, and compound-complex
simple subject : the main word in the complete subject
subject : a noun or pronoun that names whom or what a sentence is about
subordinate, or dependent, clause : a clause that cannot stand alone as a sentence because it does not express a complete thought
verb : a word used to express an action or a state of being

LEARN

Activity 1: Sentence Structure *(Offline)*

Instructions

A. Sentence Structure

Read about the kinds of sentence structure on pages L242-L244. Then do Check Your Understanding on pages L244-L245 and Connect to the Writing Process on page L245.

B. Check Your Work

When you have finished, ask an adult to check your answers to these exercises.

C. Assessment

Go online to take the assessment.

ASSESS

Lesson Checkpoint: Sentence Structure (*Online*)

It's time to check what you have learned. Go to the next screen to test your skills.

LEARN

Activity 2. Optional: Sentence Structure *(Online)*

Name ______________________ Date ______________________

Extra Practice

Sentence Structure

Sentence Structure *(pages L242–L244)*

EXERCISE B **Decide whether each sentence is simple, compound, complex, or compound-complex.**

____ **1.** The great composer Ludwig van Beethoven changed the piano and piano-playing forever.
A simple
B compound
C complex
D compound-complex

____ **2.** When pianos first became popular, they were seen as delicate instruments.
A simple
B compound
C complex
D compound-complex

____ **3.** Pianists played with a light touch and produced an even tone.
A simple
B compound
C complex
D compound-complex

____ **4.** Beethoven composed for this style at first, but then his ideas changed.
A simple
B compound
C complex
D compound-complex

____ **5.** People were astounded when he performed his music in the early 1800s.
A simple
B compound
C complex
D compound-complex

____ **6.** There were crashing chords that frightened some of his audiences, and there were extreme changes in loudness and softness.
A simple
B compound
C complex
D compound-complex

____ **7.** Beethoven sought sound effects that no one had ever thought possible.
A simple
B compound
C complex
D compound-complex

____ **8.** The demands on the piano increased, and the instrument had to be changed.
A simple
B compound
C complex
D compound-complex

____ **9.** It was not rare for pianos to break while they were being played forcefully.
A simple
B compound
C complex
D compound-complex

____ **10.** Finally the modern piano evolved, and today's pianists use instruments that can produce a wide range of sounds and stand up to strong playing.
A simple
B compound
C complex
D compound-complex

Student Guide
Lesson 7: Review

In this lesson, you will answer some review questions on what you learned in this unit about clauses. Before you take the Unit Assessment, this is your chance to find out what you do and don't know about independent clauses, subordinate clauses, and sentence structure.

Lesson Objectives

- Distinguish among adverb, adjective, and noun clauses in sentences.
- Distinguish between independent and subordinate clauses in sentences.
- Identify sentences as simple, compound, complex, or compound-complex.
- Identify the function of a relative pronoun in a sentence.
- Identify the use of a noun clause in a sentence.
- Identify the word that an adjective or adverb clause modifies.

PREPARE

Approximate lesson time is 25 minutes.

Materials

For the Student

BK English Language Handbook, Level I - pages L246-L247, L 248-L249

Optional

Extra Practice Answers

BK English Language Handbook, Level I - pages L252-L253

Keywords and Pronunciation

adjective : a word that modifies, or describes, a noun or pronoun
adjective clause : a subordinate clause that is used to modify a noun or pronoun
adjective phrase : a prepositional phrase that modifies a noun or pronoun
adverb : a word that modifies a verb, an adjective, or another adverb
adverb clause : a subordinate clause that is used mainly to modify a verb
adverb phrase : a prepositional phrase that is used to modify a verb, adjective, or adverb
antecedent (an-tuh-SEE-duhnt) : a word or group of words that a pronoun replaces, or refers to
clause : a group of words that has a subject and a verb
complex sentence : a sentence that consists of one independent clause and one or more subordinate clauses
compound sentence : two or more simple sentences, joined by a comma and coordinating conjunction or by a semicolon
compound subject : two or more subjects connected by *and* or *or* that have the same verb
compound verb : two or more verbs connected by *and* or *or* that have the same subject
compound-complex sentence : a sentence that consists of two or more independent clauses and at least one subordinate clause

dependent clause : another name for a subordinate clause
direct object : a noun or pronoun that answers the question *What?* or *Whom?* after an action verb
essential clause : a clause that is necessary to a sentence's meaning
independent, or main, clause : a clause that can stand alone as a sentence because it expresses a complete idea
indirect object : a noun or pronoun that answers the question *To or for whom?* or *To or for what?* after an action verb
main clause : another name for an independent clause
misplaced modifier : a word or phrase that seems to modify the wrong word or words because it is too far from what it describes
modifier : a word or phrase that describes or changes another word's or phrase's meaning
nonessential clause : a clause that is not necessary to a sentence's meaning
noun : a word that names a person, place, thing, or idea
noun clause : a subordinate clause that is used as a noun
object of a preposition : a noun or pronoun that follows a preposition and completes its meaning
phrase : a group of related words that acts as a single part of speech
predicate nominative : a noun or pronoun that follows a linking verb and identifies, renames, or explains the subject
preposition : a word that shows the relationship between a noun or a pronoun and another word in the sentence
pronoun : a word that takes the place of one or more nouns
relative pronoun : a pronoun that relates an adjective clause to the noun or pronoun the clause describes
sentence : a group of words that contains a subject and a verb and expresses a complete thought
sentence structure : the combination of independent and subordinate clauses in a sentence; the four different kinds of sentence structure are simple, compound, complex, and compound-complex
simple sentence : a sentence that has one subject and one verb, either or both of which may be compound
subject : a noun or pronoun that names whom or what a sentence is about
subordinate, or dependent, clause : a clause that cannot stand alone as a sentence because it does not express a complete thought
subordinating conjunction : a conjunction that introduces an adverb clause
verb : a word used to express an action or a state of being

LEARN

Activity 1: Clauses *(Offline)*

Instructions

A. Review

To prepare for the Unit Assessment, read about diagraming sentences on pages L246-L247. Then use what you have learned to complete Practice Your Skills on page L247. Then do all three of the CheckPoint exercises on pages L248-L249.

B. Check Your Work

When you have finished, have an adult check your answers. Make sure you understand the corrections for any mistakes you made. If you do that, then you should be ready for the Unit Assessment.

Activity 2: Clauses *(Offline)*

Instructions

Complete the Posttest exercise on pages L252-L253.

When you have finished, use the Extra Practice Answers page and check your answers.

Student Guide
Lesson 8: Assessment

Lesson Objectives

- Distinguish among adverb, adjective, and noun clauses in sentences.
- Distinguish between independent and subordinate clauses in sentences.
- Identify sentences as simple, compound, complex, or compound-complex.
- Identify the function of a relative pronoun in a sentence.
- Identify the use of a noun clause in a sentence.
- Identify the word that an adjective or adverb clause modifies.

PREPARE

Approximate lesson time is 25 minutes.

ASSESS

Unit Checkpoint: Clauses (*Online*)

It's time to check what you have learned. Go to the next screen to test your skills.

Student Guide
Lesson 1: Principal Parts of Verbs

Imagine trying to learn the game of chess without having names for any of the pieces! What would you call the king? That really big piece? The pawns could be "the littlest pieces." Learning to play chess would be a very awkward process indeed.

Just as the pieces of a game need names, the forms of a verb need names. This lesson on verbs will teach you those names, the principal parts of verbs. Then you'll be ready to learn how to use verb forms.

Lesson Objectives

- Identify the principal parts of regular and irregular verbs.
- Use the correct verb form to complete a sentence.

PREPARE

Approximate lesson time is 25 minutes.

Materials

For the Student

BK English Language Handbook, Level I - pages L279-L297

household items - Dictionary

Optional

Extra Practice Answers

BK English Language Handbook, Level I - page L291

Keywords and Pronunciation

irregular verb : a verb that does not form its past and past participle by adding *-ed* or *-d* to the present form
past participle : a verb form, often ending in -d or -ed; may be used as an adjective
past tense : expresses action that has already taken place or that was completed in the past
present participle : a verb form ending in -ing; may be used as an adjective
present tense : expresses action that is going on now
principal parts : the four building blocks of a verb: the present, the present participle, the past, and the past participle
regular verb : a verb that forms its past and past participle by adding *-ed* or *-d* to the present form
tense : the time expressed by a verb
usage : the ways words are employed in speaking and writing
verb : a word used to express an action or a state of being
verb forms : different ways verbs are used; usually require a change in spelling and may include the addition of a helping verb

LEARN

Activity 1: Principal Parts of Verbs *(Online)*

Activity 2: Principal Parts of Verbs *(Offline)*

Instructions

A. Regular Verbs and Irregular Verbs

Read about regular and irregular verbs on pages L279-L290. Then do items 21-30 of the Check Your Understanding exercise on page L290. Next complete Connect to the Writing Process on page L290.

B. Six Problem Verbs

Read about the six problem verbs on pages L292-L294. Then do items 11-20 of Check Your Understanding on page L295. Next, do Connect to the Writing Process on page L296. Then do QuickCheck on page L297.

Note – For Connect to the Writing Process on page L296, you need only write the correct form of the verb. Writing the entire sentence is not necessary.

C. Check Your Work

When you have finished, ask an adult to check your answers to these exercises.

D. Assessment

Go online to take the assessment.

ASSESS

Lesson Checkpoint: Principal Parts of Verbs (*Online*)

It's time to check what you have learned. Go to the next screen to test your skills.

LEARN

Activity 3. Optional: Principal Parts of Verbs *(Offline)*

Student Guide
Lesson 2: Verb Tense

Very likely, somewhere in your home is a box of old photographs. They aren't in any order. Some are black and white; some are in color. Maybe on a rainy day, you have sat on a bed, spread these pictures out, and tried to puzzle out the mysteries of the past.

What happened first? What was going on at the same time? Were you born then? To tell the story of the past, or even those stories of the present or future, you must know the order of events in time. To put that order into words, you'll need verb tenses.

Lesson Objectives

- Form and use verbs in the indicative, imperative, interrogative, conditional, and subjunctive mood.
- Identify progressive verb forms.
- Identify verb tense.
- Use the correct verb tense in a sentence.

PREPARE

Approximate lesson time is 25 minutes.

Materials

For the Student

- Verb Mood
- BK English Language Handbook, Level I - pages L298-L310

Optional

- Extra Practice Answers
- Identifying Tenses
- Progressive Verb Forms

Keywords and Pronunciation

conjugation : a list of all the singular and plural forms of a verb in all six tenses
future perfect progressive form : shows a future ongoing action that will have taken place by a stated future time
future perfect tense : expresses action that will take place before another future action or time
future progressive form : shows an ongoing action that will take place in the future
future tense : expresses action that will take place in the future
helping verb : an auxiliary verb that helps to make up a verb phrase
irregular verb : a verb that does not form its past and past participle by adding *-ed* or *-d* to the present form
past participle : a verb form, often ending in -d or -ed; may be used as an adjective
past perfect progressive form : shows a past ongoing action that was interrupted by another past action
past perfect tense : expresses action that took place before some other past action
past progressive form : shows an ongoing action that took place in the past
past tense : expresses action that has already taken place or that was completed in the past

present participle : a verb form ending in -ing; may be used as an adjective
present perfect progressive form : shows an ongoing action that is continuing in the present
present perfect tense : expresses action that was completed at some indefinite time in the past or that has started in the past and is still going on
present progressive form : shows an ongoing action that is taking place now
present tense : expresses action that is going on now
principal parts : the four building blocks of a verb: the present, the present participle, the past, and the past participle
progressive verb form : verb used to express continuing or ongoing action; progressive forms are composed of a form of the verb be and the present participle.
regular verb : a verb that forms its past and past participle by adding *-ed* or *-d* to the present form
tense : the time expressed by a verb
verb : a word used to express an action or a state of being

LEARN

Activity 1: Verb Tense *(Offline)*

Instructions

A. Verb Tense, Verb Conjugation

Read about verb tense and verb conjugation on pages L298-L304. Then do two Check Your Understanding exercises: one on page L304 and the other on page L305. Next do Connect to the Writing Process on pages L305-L306.

B. Progressive Verb Forms

Read about progressive verb forms on pages L307-L310. Then do Check Your Understanding on pages L308-L309.

C. Verb Mood

Verbs not only have tense, but they also have mood. Read the information and examples on the Verb Mood page and complete the exercises.

D. Check Your Work

When you have finished, ask an adult to check your answers to these exercises.

E. Assessment

Go online to take the assessment.

ASSESS

Lesson Checkpoint: Verb Tense (*Online*)

It's time to check what you have learned. Go to the next screen to test your skills.

LEARN

Activity 2. Optional: Verb Tense *(Online)*

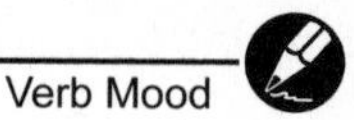

Verb Mood

Just as a verb has tense, a verb also has mood. In grammar, the mood of a verb shows the writer's or speaker's attitude toward what he or she is saying.

The three main moods of verbs are the indicative, imperative, and subjunctive moods. The interrogative mood is a special form of the indicative mood. The conditional mood is a special form of the subjunctive mood.

Indicative Mood

The indicative mood is used to express facts or opinions.

> Your house is very big.
>
> The sunset was extremely beautiful.

The indicative mood is the most common mood in English.

The **interrogative mood**, a form of the indicative mood, is used to ask questions.

> Do you have an extra pencil?
>
> Can we go to the movies later?

Imperative Mood

The imperative mood is used to express commands and direct requests.

> Stop singing that song!
>
> Give me that picture.

Tip: It may seem as if the imperative mood doesn't have a subject, but it does. The subject is *you*, although it isn't stated.

Subjunctive Mood

The subjunctive mood is used to express uncertainty, wishes, requirements, or suggestions.

> The tutor urged that the student consider submitting a poem to the literary magazine.
>
> I move that the last comment be struck from the record.

The subjunctive mood has become fairly uncommon in English.

The **conditional mood**, a form of the subjunctive mood, expresses possibility or a condition contrary to fact. One clause in the sentence generally begins with the word *if*, while the other clause usually has a verb phrase with a helping verb such as *would*, *could*, or *may*.

> If I had two dollars, I would buy a comic book.
>
> If it stops raining, I may go to the park.

Identify the mood of the verb in each sentence.

1. Stop eating my french fries.

   A. Indicative
   B. Imperative
   C. Subjunctive
   D. Interrogative
   E. Conditional

2. If I were taller, I would play basketball.

   A. Indicative
   B. Imperative
   C. Subjunctive
   D. Interrogative
   E. Conditional

3. The moon is very bright tonight.

   A. Indicative
   B. Imperative
   C. Subjunctive
   D. Interrogative
   E. Conditional

4. Have you seen my red boots?

   A. Indicative
   B. Imperative
   C. Subjunctive
   D. Interrogative
   E. Conditional

5. I suggested that he read the assignment more carefully in the future.

   A. Indicative
   B. Imperative
   C. Subjunctive
   D. Interrogative
   E. Conditional

6. Don't open that door.

   A. Indicative
   B. Imperative
   C. Subjunctive
   D. Interrogative
   E. Conditional

7. You are late for your swimming lesson.

   A. Indicative
   B. Imperative
   C. Subjunctive
   D. Interrogative
   E. Conditional

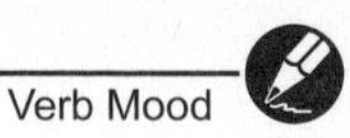

Rewrite the sentences to change the mood of the verb.

1. Rewrite the sentence so the verb is changed from the indicative mood to the interrogative mood.
   The cat is sitting in the oak tree.

   ____

2. Rewrite the sentence so the verb is changed from the indicative mood to the imperative mood.
   You are putting down the basketball.

   ____

3. Rewrite the sentence so the verb is changed from the conditional mood to the indicative mood.
   If I were a good singer, I might be in a band.

   ____

Name ____________________ Date ____________________

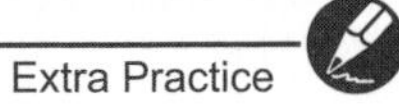

Identifying Tenses

Identifying Tenses *(pages L298–L304)*

EXERCISE Choose the correct tense of the underlined verb.

____**22.** Will you sneeze during class today?
A past perfect
B future

____**23.** What color are your socks?
A future
B present

____**24.** By 5:30 this evening, how long will you have been awake?
A future perfect
B future

____**25.** Was there anything green in your closet this morning?
A past perfect
B past

____**26.** The Winter Olympics provides skaters with an ideal opportunity.
A present
B future perfect

____**27.** Every pair hopes for a gold medal for their performance.
A past
B present

____**28.** Years of preparation and rehearsal lie behind each act.
A present
B past perfect

____**29.** Jayne Torvill and Christopher Dean entered the Winter Olympics in Yugoslavia.
A future
B past

____**30.** They represented Great Britain in the figure skating events.
A past
B past perfect

____**31.** Before the judges and audience, they performed a beautiful dance.
A present
B past

____**32.** For the first time, a skating routine earned a perfect score.
A past
B future

____**33.** The English people remember Torvill and Dean with great pride.
A past
B present

____**34.** Future Olympics will provide other skaters with gold medals.
A future
B past

____**35.** Before the phonograph most people had heard only live music.
A perfect
B past perfect

____**36.** By 1930, most Americans had listened to phonograph records.
A past perfect
B present perfect

____**37.** During World War II, juke boxes had become popular.
A present perfect
B past perfect

____**38.** Nowadays everyone has listened to music in banks, stores, and even dentists' offices.
A past perfect
B present perfect

____**39.** Today people test the effect of music on plants.
A past
B present

Name ____________________ Date ____________________

Extra Practice

Progressive Verb Forms

Progressive Verb Forms *(pages L307–L308)*

EXERCISE C Complete each sentence by choosing the verb form in parentheses.

____ **1.** Until now, I _____ well. (past perfect progressive)
A was performing
B am performing
C had been performing
D will be performing

____ **2.** We _____ a garage sale. (present progressive)
A were having
B had been having
C are having
D will be having

____ **3.** Captain Galdamez _____ the jet. (future progressive)
A has been flying
B will be flying
C had been flying
D was flying

____ **4.** Sonny _____ homework for two hours. (present perfect progressive)
A has been doing
B will have been doing
C had been doing
D was doing

____ **5.** She _____ when she broke her leg. (past progressive)
A is skiing
B has been skiing
C had been skiing
D was skiing

____ **6.** By five o'clock, we _____ for three hours. (future perfect progressive)
A were practicing
B have been practicing
C will have been practicing
D had been practicing

____ **7.** I _____ the floor when I found the bracelet. (past progressive)
A had been sweeping
B was sweeping
C will have been sweeping
D am sweeping

____ **8.** The principal _____ us. (present perfect progressive)
A will be encouraging
B was encouraging
C is encouraging
D has been encouraging

____ **9.** Nadia _____ her hair. (present progressive)
A is styling
B was styling
C will be styling
D will have been styling

____ **10.** Leon _____ the stars through a telescope. (past perfect progressive)
A had been studying
B was studying
C will have been studying
D is studying

____ **11.** We _____ till the band goes home. (future progressive)
A are dancing
B were dancing
C will be dancing
D have been dancing

____ **12.** By February, Keisha _____ as class president for six months. (future perfect progressive)
A is serving
B will have been serving
C had been serving
D has been serving.

Student Guide
Lesson 3: Shifts in Tense

Have you ever been at a fancy restaurant, looked down, and discovered that your socks don't match? Or worse: your shoes don't match! Maybe you quickly hid your feet under a table and hoped that nobody would notice. Maybe no one did; then again, maybe there was someone who had a sly smile and seemed to know.

Shifts in tense are like mismatched shoes. Yes, people do notice, and knowing that someone will notice your blunder can be embarrassing. However, in one way, shifts in tense are worse than a fashion mistake: they can also confuse people.

Lesson Objectives

- Correct verb tense shifts in sentences.
- Recognize verb tense shifts in sentences.

PREPARE

Approximate lesson time is 25 minutes.

Materials

For the Student

BK English Language Handbook, Level I - pages L310-L313

Optional

Extra Practice Answers

Shifts in Tense

Keywords and Pronunciation

shift in tense : an unnecessary and confusing change in verb tense within a sentence or a group of related sentences

tense : the time expressed by a verb

LEARN

Activity 1: Shifts in Tense *(Offline)*

Instructions

A. Shifts in Tense

Read about shifts in tense on pages L310-L311. Then do Check Your Understanding on pages L311-L312. Next complete QuickCheck on page L313.

B. Check Your Work

When you have finished, ask an adult to check your answers to these exercises.

C. Assessment

Go online to take the assessment.

ASSESS

Lesson Checkpoint: Shifts in Tense (*Online*)

It's time to check what you have learned. Go to the next screen to test your skills.

LEARN

Activity 2. Optional: Shifts in Tense *(Online)*

Name _______________ Date _______________

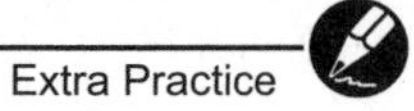

Shifts in Tense

CHAPTER 10 Shifts in Tense *(pages L310–L311)*

EXERCISE A **Decide whether each sentence has an unnecessary and incorrect shift in verb tense.**

____ **1.** That large motorboat always slows down before it stopped at the dock.
A yes
B no

____ **2.** Chris walked bravely to the front of the room and faces his classmates.
A yes
B no

____ **3.** The kitten stalked into the room and pounced on the rubber mouse.
A yes
B no

____ **4.** After I had begun to mow the lawn, the rain starts.
A yes
B no

____ **5.** The sightseeing boat leaves at noon and returned at three o'clock.
A yes
B no

____ **6.** The halfback lost his balance but hung onto the ball.
A yes
B no

____ **7.** Huge jets always pass directly over our house and headed west.
A yes
B no

____ **8.** When Cider ran away, Ken searches for him everywhere.
A yes
B no

____ **9.** I had played the video game before I order it.
A yes
B no

____ **10.** After I had seen the movie, I told everyone about it.
A yes
B no

____ **11.** I walked into the restaurant and see a beautiful girl.
A yes
B no

____ **12.** Last week we were camping and catch fish for our dinner.
A yes
B no

____ **13.** Each evening the wind blows through the trees and rattled my window.
A yes
B no

____ **14.** I dug in my locker and want to find the small notebook.
A yes
B no

____ **15.** We park the car at the curb and jump out.
A yes
B no

____ **16.** My grandmother gives me a necklace, and I lost it.
A yes
B no

____ **17.** Modern baseball was once named town ball, and it first become popular in the United States in the 1830s.
A yes
B no

____ **18.** Wooden stakes are the bases, and the playing field was square.
A yes
B no

Name ____________________ Date ____________________

Extra Practice

Shifts in Tense

Shifts in Tense *(pages L310–L311)*

EXERCISE B **Choose the word group that completes the sentence without an incorrect shift in tense.**

____ **1.** I was reading a story
A and notice a spider on my arm.
B and noticed a spider on my arm.

____ **2.** The girls call their moms
A and then are going to the movie.
B and then go to the movie.

____ **3.** Sometimes I yell at a friend
A and then felt bad.
B and then feel bad.

____ **4.** I built a sandcastle,
A but the waves demolished it.
B but the waves demolish it.

____ **5.** Ms. Garber said we could take the test immediately,
A or we were reviewing first.
B or we could review first.

____ **6.** The dog was yelping,
A so I knew something was wrong.
B so I knew something is wrong.

____ **7.** The war ended,
A and peace reigned.
B and peace was reigning.

____ **8.** I looked across the cafeteria,
A but I see no one to sit with.
B but I saw no one to sit with.

____ **9.** Show me the math problem,
A and I will help you with it.
B and I help you with it.

____ **10.** When the vehicle was new,
A it had shiny white paint.
B it was having shiny white paint.

____ **11.** The drummer has suggested a change in the song,
A and the other band members agree.
B and the other band members agreed.

____ **12.** I was laughing so hard
A that tears will be running out of my eyes.
B that tears were running out of my eyes.

____ **13.** When darkness fell,
A the lights on the pier came on.
B the lights on the pier come on.

____ **14.** We can either ride the Ferris wheel
A or get some cotton candy.
B or getting some cotton candy.

____ **15.** The hermit crab searched for a bigger shell,
A yet no empty one has been in sight.
B yet no empty one was in sight.

Student Guide
Lesson 4: Active and Passive Voice

Picture this: you have just shattered the lamp that your great-grandmother gave your mother on her wedding day. You hear a key in the front door's lock. Your mother is home!

Do you say, "Mom, I broke your lamp"? Or, in a more diplomatic fashion, do you say, "Mom, I'm sorry to tell you that your lamp was broken"?

If you don't want to emphasize your active role in the lamp's tragic end, you'll use the passive voice.

Lesson Objectives

- Distinguish between active voice and passive voice verbs in sentences.
- Recognize and correct inappropriate shifts in verb mood.
- Recognize and correct inappropriate shifts in verb voice.
- Recognize the voice of verbs.
- Use verbs in the active and passive voice to achieve particular effects.
- Use verbs in the conditional and subjunctive mood to achieve particular effects.

PREPARE

Approximate lesson time is 25 minutes.

Materials

For the Student

- Inappropriate Shifts in Voice and Mood
- Using Mood
- Using Voice
- BK English Language Handbook, Level I - pages L314-L316

Optional

- Active and Passive Voice
- Extra Practice Answers

Keywords and Pronunciation

active voice : indicates the subject is performing the action
direct object : a noun or pronoun that answers the question *What?* or *Whom?* after an action verb
passive voice : indicates that the action of the verb is being performed on the subject
past participle : a verb form, often ending in -d or -ed; may be used as an adjective
subject : a noun or pronoun that names whom or what a sentence is about
transitive verb : an action verb that has a direct object
verb : a word used to express an action or a state of being

LEARN

Activity 1: Active and Passive Voice *(Offline)*

Shifts in voice, as well as shifts in mood, can result in unclear and ineffective writing. Understanding verb voice and verb mood will help students continue to become strong communicators.

Instructions

A. Use of Active and Passive Voice

Read about active and passive voice on pages L314-L315. Then do Check Your Understanding on pages L315-L316. Next, do Connect to the Writing Process on page L316.

B. Inappropriate Shifts in Voice and Mood

Learn about inappropriate shifts in voice and mood. Read the information and examples on the Inappropriate Shifts in Voice and Mood page and complete the exercises.

C. Using Mood

Learn about how to use mood to create effects. Read the information and examples on the Using Mood page and complete the exercise.

D. Check Your Work

When you have finished, ask an adult to check your answers to these exercises.

E. Assessment

Go online to take the assessment.

ASSESS

Lesson Checkpoint: Active and Passive Voice (*Online*)

It's time to check what you have learned. Go to the next screen to test your skills.

LEARN

Activity 2. Optional: Active and Passive Voice *(Online)*

Inappropriate Shifts in Voice and Mood

The voice and mood of verbs should be consistent in a sentence.

Inappropriate Shifts in Voice

Avoid changing between the active voice and the passive voice within a sentence.

> **Incorrect:** As we walked past the diner, our friends' calls were heard through the window.
>
> **Correct:** As we walked past the diner, we heard our friends' calls through the window. (Both verbs are in the active voice.)

In general, you should change both verbs to active voice, even if the verb in the passive voice comes first in the sentence.

> **Incorrect:** The uniforms were brought by our coach, and we put them on.
>
> **Correct:** Our coach brought the uniforms, and we put them on. (Both verbs are in the active voice.)

Rewrite the sentence to eliminate the inappropriate shift in voice.

1. I threw the ball, and it was caught by the dog.

   ____

2. Tommy bought the popcorn, but it was eaten by Amelia.

   ____

3. The door was closed by my brother, and my sister knocked on it.

   ____

4. My mother painted the canvas, and then it was set on the easel to dry.

   ____

5. The car was washed by our neighbor, but he didn't wax it.

   ____

6. Esteban looked through the telescope, and a shooting star was seen by him.

   ____

Inappropriate Shifts in Mood

Avoid changing the mood of a verb within a sentence.

Incorrect: Collect magazines, and you should make a collage with them. (The first verb is in the imperative mood, the second is in the indicative mood.)

Correct: Collect magazines and make a collage with them. (Both verbs are in the imperative mood.)

Correct: You should collect magazines, and you should make a collage with them. (Both verbs are in the indicative mood.)

Rewrite the sentence to eliminate the inappropriate shift in mood.

1. Run to the garage, and you should check to see if the bike is there.

 ____

2. Stir the flour into the mixture, but you shouldn't add the eggs yet.

 ____

3. The librarian asked that we lower our voices and she wants us to stop running as well.

 ____

4. If the rain were to continue, we will have a a flood.

 ____

 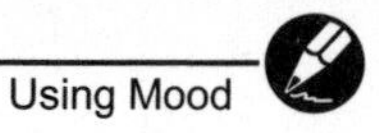

Using Mood

Just as good writers know how to use voice to achieve a certain effect, they also need to know how to use mood.

Subjunctive and Conditional Moods

A writer can choose to use the subjunctive mood or the conditional mood to change the emphasis of a sentence. It can be very effective in turning a simple statement into a more complex statement that shows possibility and imagines a different set of circumstances.

Clean your room. (The imperative mood makes a direct, strong statement.)

I suggest that you clean your room. (The subjunctive mood is less direct. It sounds more polite.)

I can't get enough done. (The indicative mood makes a simple statement.)

I could get everything done if the day were 40 hours long. (With the conditional mood, the writer can expand upon the original statement by imagining a different possibility, something contrary to fact.)

Change the sentence from the indicative mood to the conditional mood to create a statement contrary to the fact.

1. The soup isn't finished, so we aren't eating yet.

   ____

2. I'm not very tall, so I can't play basketball.

   ____

Change the sentence from the indicative mood to the subjunctive mood to create a different effect.

3. Her mother told Cindy to change her shoes.

   ____

4. Blaire asked to be my friend.

   ____

Using Voice

Compare these sentences:

Active voice: Alex rode the bicycle.

Passive voice: The bicycle was ridden by Alex.

The sentence in the active voice is shorter and more direct. The sentence in the active voice emphasizes the subject, Alex. In general, use active voice when you write.

Sometimes, however, it's appropriate to use the passive voice. Compare these sentences:

Active voice: Abby found Sarah putting on her mother's makeup.

Passive voice: Sarah was found putting on her mother's makeup.

If you want to emphasize that Abby found Sarah, then active voice is better. But if you want to emphasize that Sarah was found, passive voice is better. The fact that Abby found Sarah may not be important.

Read these sentences:

Active voice: Ice coated the tree branches.

Passive voice: The tree branches were coated with ice.

The sentence in the active voice emphasizes the ice. The sentence in the passive voice emphasizes the branches. The choice of active or passive voice depends on what the writer wants to emphasize.

Rewrite the sentence in the active voice. Explain how the meaning changes.

1. The ballad was sung beautifully by Gina.

____

____

Rewrite the sentence in the passive voice. Explain how the meaning changes.

2. Mr. Jackson discovered a dinosaur bone in the park.

____

____

CHAPTER 10 Active and Passive Voice *(pages L314–L315)*

EXERCISE **Decide whether each sentence is written in active voice or passive voice.**

____ **1.** Ancient ruins have been discovered in our backyard.
A active voice
B passive voice

____ **2.** The White House has 132 rooms.
A active voice
B passive voice

____ **3.** Some businesses are guarded at night by watchdogs.
A active voice
B passive voice

____ **4.** Jupiter's moons can be seen with good binoculars.
A active voice
B passive voice

____ **5.** Dry the dishes with that towel.
A active voice
B passive voice

____ **6.** The Gulf Stream warms the west coast of Europe.
A active voice
B passive voice

____ **7.** The dog left a trail of muddy footprints.
A active voice
B passive voice

____ **8.** Jade can be shattered by a sharp blow.
A active voice
B passive voice

____ **9.** Tonight I must write a report for science class.
A active voice
B passive voice

____ **10.** Computers are used to predict the monthly rainfall over the next five years.
A active voice
B passive voice

____ **11.** James is always called Jim by his family.
A active voice
B passive voice

____ **12.** Did you plant those tulips yourself?
A active voice
B passive voice

____ **13.** The lead part was played by Jayne.
A active voice
B passive voice

____ **14.** My report on solar energy will be finished soon.
A active voice
B passive voice

____ **15.** A terrible thunderstorm followed the rain.
A active voice
B passive voice

____ **16.** Bart found two dimes under the cushions of the sofa.
A active voice
B passive voice

____ **17.** The wedding vows were written by the couple.
A active voice
B passive voice

____ **18.** Many deer chew the bark on our trees.
A active voice
B passive voice

____ **19.** Joshua made a lamp for his mother.
A active voice
B passive voice

____ **20.** The kitchen window was broken this afternoon.
A active voice
B passive voice

Student Guide
Lesson 5: Review

In this lesson, you will answer some review questions on what you learned in this unit about using verbs. Before you take the Unit Assessment, this is your chance to find out what you do and don't know about using verbs, including identifying the principal parts of verbs, using regular and irregular verbs, using the six problem verbs, identifying verb tenses and shifts in tense, and using active voice and passive voice.

Lesson Objectives

- Distinguish between active voice and passive voice verbs in sentences.
- Identify progressive verb forms.
- Identify the principal parts of regular and irregular verbs.
- Identify verb tense.
- Recognize and correct verb tense shifts in sentences.
- Use the correct form of a verb to complete a sentence.

PREPARE

Approximate lesson time is 25 minutes.

Materials

For the Student

BK English Language Handbook, Level I - pages L317-L319

Optional

Extra Practice Answers

BK English Language Handbook, Level I - pages L322-L323

Keywords and Pronunciation

active voice : indicates the subject is performing the action
conjugation : a list of all the singular and plural forms of a verb in all six tenses
direct object : a noun or pronoun that answers the question *What?* or *Whom?* after an action verb
future perfect progressive form : shows a future ongoing action that will have taken place by a stated future time
future perfect tense : expresses action that will take place before another future action or time
future progressive form : shows an ongoing action that will take place in the future
future tense : expresses action that will take place in the future
helping verb : an auxiliary verb that helps to make up a verb phrase
irregular verb : a verb that does not form its past and past participle by adding *-ed* or *-d* to the present form
passive voice : indicates that the action of the verb is being performed on the subject
past participle : a verb form, often ending in -d or -ed; may be used as an adjective
past perfect progressive form : shows a past ongoing action that was interrupted by another past action
past perfect tense : expresses action that took place before some other past action
past progressive form : shows an ongoing action that took place in the past
past tense : expresses action that has already taken place or that was completed in the past

present participle : the second principal part of a verb; ends in -ing and is used for all six tenses of progressive verb forms
present perfect progressive form : shows an ongoing action that is continuing in the present
present perfect tense : expresses action that was completed at some indefinite time in the past or that has started in the past and is still going on
present progressive form : shows an ongoing action that is taking place now
present tense : expresses action that is going on now
principal parts : the four building blocks of a verb: the present, the present participle, the past, and the past participle
progressive verb form : verb used to express continuing or ongoing action; progressive forms are composed of a form of the verb be and the present participle.
regular verb : a verb that forms its past and past participle by adding *-ed* or *-d* to the present form
shift in tense : an unnecessary and confusing change in verb tense within a sentence or a group of related sentences
subject : a noun or pronoun that names whom or what a sentence is about
tense : the time expressed by a verb
transitive verb : an action verb that has a direct object
verb : a word used to express an action or a state of being
verb forms : different ways verbs are used; usually require a change in spelling and may include the addition of a helping verb

---

LEARN

Activity 1: Using Verbs *(Offline)*

Instructions

A. Review

To prepare for the Unit Assessment, complete QuickCheck on page L317 and Using the Correct Verb Form and Understanding Tenses in the CheckPoint exercises on pages L318-L319.

B. Check Your Work

When you have finished, have an adult check your answers. Make sure you understand the corrections for any mistakes you made. If you do that, then you should be ready for the Unit Assessment.

Activity 2. Optional: Using Verbs *(Offline)*

Instructions

Extra Practice: Complete the Posttest exercise on pages L322-L323.

When you have finished, use the Extra Practice Answers page and check your answers.

Shifts in Tense

CHAPTER 10 Shifts in Tense *(pages L310–L311)*

EXERCISE A Decide whether each sentence has an unnecessary and incorrect shift in verb tense.

____ **1.** That large motorboat always slows down before it stopped at the dock.
A yes
B no

____ **2.** Chris walked bravely to the front of the room and faces his classmates.
A yes
B no

____ **3.** The kitten stalked into the room and pounced on the rubber mouse.
A yes
B no

____ **4.** After I had begun to mow the lawn, the rain starts.
A yes
B no

____ **5.** The sightseeing boat leaves at noon and returned at three o'clock.
A yes
B no

____ **6.** The halfback lost his balance but hung onto the ball.
A yes
B no

____ **7.** Huge jets always pass directly over our house and headed west.
A yes
B no

____ **8.** When Cider ran away, Ken searches for him everywhere.
A yes
B no

____ **9.** I had played the video game before I order it.
A yes
B no

____ **10.** After I had seen the movie, I told everyone about it.
A yes
B no

____ **11.** I walked into the restaurant and see a beautiful girl.
A yes
B no

____ **12.** Last week we were camping and catch fish for our dinner.
A yes
B no

____ **13.** Each evening the wind blows through the trees and rattled my window.
A yes
B no

____ **14.** I dug in my locker and want to find the small notebook.
A yes
B no

____ **15.** We park the car at the curb and jump out.
A yes
B no

____ **16.** My grandmother gives me a necklace, and I lost it.
A yes
B no

____ **17.** Modern baseball was once named town ball, and it first become popular in the United States in the 1830s.
A yes
B no

____ **18.** Wooden stakes are the bases, and the playing field was square.
A yes
B no

Shifts in Tense

Shifts in Tense *(pages L310–L311)*

EXERCISE B **Choose the word group that completes the sentence without an incorrect shift in tense.**

____ **1.** I was reading a story
A and notice a spider on my arm.
B and noticed a spider on my arm.

____ **2.** The girls call their moms
A and then are going to the movie.
B and then go to the movie.

____ **3.** Sometimes I yell at a friend
A and then felt bad.
B and then feel bad.

____ **4.** I built a sandcastle,
A but the waves demolished it.
B but the waves demolish it.

____ **5.** Ms. Garber said we could take the test immediately,
A or we were reviewing first.
B or we could review first.

____ **6.** The dog was yelping,
A so I knew something was wrong.
B so I knew something is wrong.

____ **7.** The war ended,
A and peace reigned.
B and peace was reigning.

____ **8.** I looked across the cafeteria,
A but I see no one to sit with.
B but I saw no one to sit with.

____ **9.** Show me the math problem,
A and I will help you with it.
B and I help you with it.

____ **10.** When the vehicle was new,
A it had shiny white paint.
B it was having shiny white paint.

____ **11.** The drummer has suggested a change in the song,
A and the other band members agree.
B and the other band members agreed.

____ **12.** I was laughing so hard
A that tears will be running out of my eyes.
B that tears were running out of my eyes.

____ **13.** When darkness fell,
A the lights on the pier came on.
B the lights on the pier come on.

____ **14.** We can either ride the Ferris wheel
A or get some cotton candy.
B or getting some cotton candy.

____ **15.** The hermit crab searched for a bigger shell,
A yet no empty one has been in sight.
B yet no empty one was in sight.

Student Guide
Lesson 6: Assessment

Lesson Objectives

- Distinguish between active voice and passive voice verbs in sentences.
- Identify progressive verb forms.
- Identify the principal parts of regular and irregular verbs.
- Identify verb tense.
- Recognize and correct verb tense shifts in sentences.
- Use the correct form of a verb to complete a sentence.

PREPARE

Approximate lesson time is 25 minutes.

ASSESS

Unit Checkpoint: Using Verbs (*Online*)

It's time to check what you have learned. Go to the next screen to test your skills.

Student Guide
Lesson 1: Semester Review

Lesson Objectives

- Identify the function of a relative pronoun in a sentence.
- Identify the principal parts of regular and irregular verbs.
- Demonstrate mastery of important knowledge and skills learned in this semester.

PREPARE

Approximate lesson time is 25 minutes.

LEARN
Activity 1: Literary Analysis and Composition - GUM *(Online)*

Student Guide
Lesson 2: Semester Assessment

Lesson Objectives

- Distinguish among adverb, adjective, and noun clauses in sentences.
- Distinguish among the four kinds of complements.
- Distinguish between active voice and passive voice verbs in sentences.
- Distinguish between correctly placed and misplaced or dangling modifiers.
- Distinguish between independent and subordinate clauses in sentences.
- Distinguish between sentence fragments and complete sentences.
- Distinguish between sentences and run-on sentences.
- Identify adjective, adverb, and appositive phrases and the words they modify or rename in sentences.
- Identify gerunds and gerund phrases and their uses in sentences.
- Identify infinitives and infinitive phrases and their uses in sentences.
- Identify participles and participial phrases and the words they modify in sentences.
- Identify sentences as simple, compound, complex, or compound-complex.
- Identify subjects and verbs in sentences in natural and inverted order.
- Identify the use of a noun clause in a sentence.
- Identify the word that an adjective or adverb clause modifies.
- Identify verb tense.
- Identify verbals and verbal phrases in sentences.
- Recognize and correct verb tense shifts in sentences.
- Use the correct form of a verb to complete a sentence.

PREPARE

Approximate lesson time is 25 minutes.

ASSESS

Semester Assessment: Semester Review and Assessment (*Online*)

It's time to check what you have learned. Go to the next screen to test your skills.

Student Guide
Lesson 1: Pronoun Case

Most people take their names quite seriously. Perhaps you're one of them. How would you react if someone called you by the wrong name? At first, you'd probably smile and simply correct the error. Then, if the person kept repeating the error, you might well begin to avoid the person altogether.

Pronouns take the place of nouns like names. If you think those little words like *he, she,* and *it* don't matter, try calling someone an *it* or referring to a girl as *he*. These small errors can have big consequences.

In this lesson, you'll learn how to use pronouns correctly.

Lesson Objectives

- Distinguish between possessive pronouns and contractions.
- Identify objective case pronouns as direct objects, indirect objects, or objects of prepositions in sentences.
- Use the correct nominative case pronouns to complete sentences.
- Use the correct objective case pronouns to complete sentences.
- Use the correct possessive case pronouns to complete sentences.
- Use the correct pronoun case to complete sentences.

PREPARE

Approximate lesson time is 25 minutes.

Materials

For the Student

BK English Language Handbook, Level I - pages L327-L345

Optional

Extra Practice Answers

BK English Language Handbook, Level I - page L345

Keywords and Pronunciation

case : a form of a noun or a pronoun that indicates its use in a sentence; in English there are three cases: the nominative case, the objective case, and the possessive case
contraction : the shortened form of two or more words, with an apostrophe to replace missing letters
nominative case : noun or pronoun forms used for subjects and predicate nominatives
objective case : the noun or pronoun forms used for direct objects, indirect objects, or objects of prepositions
possessive case : noun or pronoun forms used to show ownership or possession
pronoun : a word that takes the place of one or more nouns

LEARN

Activity 1: Pronoun Case *(Online)*

Activity 2: Pronoun Case *(Offline)*

Instructions

A. Nominative Case

Read about case and nominative case pronouns on pages L327-L333. Then do sections of two Check Your Understanding exercises. Do items 1-10 of the first one, on page L331. Then do items 6-15 of the second exercise, on pages L333-L334. Next complete Connect to the Writing Process on page L335.

Note – For Connect to the Writing Process on page L335, you need only write the incorrect pronoun and the correction. There is no need to write out the sentences in this exercise.

B. Objective Case

Read about objective case pronouns on pages L335-L338. Then do items 16-25 of Check Your Understanding on page L339. Next do QuickCheck on page L341.

C. Possessive Case

Read about possessive case pronouns on pages L341-L342. Then do two Check Your Understanding exercises: items 6-10 of the first exercise on page L343 and items 11-17 of the second exercise on the same page. Next, complete Connect to the Writing Process on page L344.

D. Check Your Work

When you have finished, ask an adult to check your answers to these exercises.

E. Assessment

Go online to take the assessment.

ASSESS

Lesson Checkpoint: Pronoun Case (*Online*)

It's time to check what you have learned. Go to the next screen to test your skills.

LEARN

Activity 3. Optional: Pronoun Case *(Online)*

Student Guide
Lesson 2: Pronoun Problems

Have you ever known a set of identical twins? Confusing, isn't it? But after a while, you begin to notice things. Jed, for instance, has thicker eyebrows than Ed. Perhaps, Sarah has a freckle on the end of her nose, and Sally doesn't. At first, you are able to tell one twin from the other only when you see them together. Then, before you know it, you can recognize each twin alone.

Learning when to use *who* and when to use *whom* is much the same experience. Once you recognize the characteristics of each form, you'll soon have no trouble identifying who is who.

Lesson Objectives

- Identify the use of *who* and its related forms in sentences.
- Use the correct form of *who* to complete sentences.
- Identify the use of who and its related forms in sentences.
- Use the correct form of who to complete sentences.

PREPARE

Approximate lesson time is 25 minutes.

Materials

For the Student

Who and Whom in Questions

BK English Language Handbook, Level I - pages L346-L350

Optional

Extra Practice Answers

BK English Language Handbook, Level I - pages L350-L351

Keywords and Pronunciation

adjective clause : a subordinate clause that is used to modify a noun or pronoun
clause : a group of words that has a subject and a verb
nominative case : noun or pronoun forms used for subjects and predicate nominatives
noun clause : a subordinate clause that is used as a noun
objective case : the noun or pronoun forms used for direct objects, indirect objects, or objects of prepositions
possessive case : noun or pronoun forms used to show ownership or possession

LEARN

Activity 1: Pronoun Problems *(Offline)*

Instructions

A. *Who* or *Whom?* in Questions

Read about using *who* and *whom* in questions on pages L346-L347. Then do the Choosing Between *Who* and *Whom* in Questions page.

Note – Remember that questions use inverted sentence structure. For example, when rephrased in natural order, the question *Who is the captain?* becomes *The captain is who? Who* is the predicate nominative in this sentence.

B. *Who* or *Whom?* in Clauses

Read about using *who* and *whom* in clauses on pages L348-L349. Then do Check Your Understanding on page L349. Next complete Connect to the Writing Process on page L350.

C. Check Your Work

When you have finished, ask an adult to check your answers to these exercises.

D. Assessment

Go online to take the assessment.

ASSESS

Lesson Checkpoint: Pronoun Problems (*Online*)

It's time to check what you have learned. Go to the next screen to test your skills.

LEARN

Activity 2. Optional: Pronoun Problems *(Online)*

Name Date 

Choosing Between *Who* and *Whom* in Questions

Underline the correct form of the pronoun. After each sentence, write how the pronoun is used in the sentence.

1. (*Who, Whom*) found my wallet?

2. To (*who, whom*) did you address the letter?

3. (*Who, Whom*) have the voters elected?

4. With (*who, whom*) are you going to the party?

5. In this case, (*who, whom*) is correct?

6. On (*who, whom*) is the main character based?

7. (*Who, Whom*) did you meet there?

8. (*Who, Whom*) is your role model?

9. (*Who, Whom*) was known by the pen name Mark Twain?

10. (*Who, Whom*) did the manager hire?

Student Guide
Lesson 3: Pronouns in Comparison

The abilities to say little and to understand what is not said are highly prized by English speakers. Just think of the many sayings that praise these skills: the less said the better; silence is golden; never wink when a nod will do; and brevity is the soul of wit.

Perhaps, English speakers must "read between the lines" because English uses many elliptical clauses. In this lesson, you'll learn that the words you leave out may influence the pronouns you choose.

Lesson Objectives

- Use pronouns that agree with their antecedents in sentences.
- Use the correct pronoun in elliptical clauses in sentences.

PREPARE

Approximate lesson time is 25 minutes.

Materials

For the Student

BK English Language Handbook, Level I - pages L351-L357

Optional

Extra Practice Answers

Pronouns and Their Antecedents

Pronouns in Comparisons

Keywords and Pronunciation

antecedent (an-tuh-SEE-duhnt) : a word or group of words that a pronoun replaces, or refers to
comparison : a group of words that describes similarities or differences between two or more people or things
elliptical clause : a subordinate clause in which words are omitted but understood to be there
gender : classification according to sex: masculine, feminine, or neuter (neither)
number : classification of a word as singular (one) or plural (more than one)

LEARN
Activity 1: Pronouns in Comparison *(Offline)*

Instructions

A. Pronouns in Comparison

Read about using pronouns in comparisons on pages L351-L352. Then do Check Your Understanding on page L353, items 16-25.

Note – You do not have to write the complete sentence. You may write the correct pronoun and then write the rest of the elliptical clause.

B. Pronouns and Their Antecedents.

Read about pronouns and their antecedents on pages L355-L356. Then do Check Your Understanding on page L357.

C. Check Your Work

When you have finished, ask an adult to check your answers to these exercises.

D. Assessment

Go online to take the assessment.

ASSESS

Lesson Checkpoint: Pronouns in Comparison (*Online*)

It's time to check what you have learned. Go to the next screen to test your skills.

LEARN

Activity 2. Optional: Pronouns in Comparison *(Online)*

Name Date

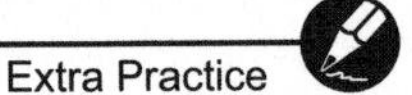

Pronouns and Their Antecedents

Write the pronoun that agrees with its antecedent in each sentence. Do not use *you.*

1. The boy and his little sister walked quickly through the trees on _____ way home.
2. This would be the perfect opportunity for a girl like ____.
3. What a show Mary and Carol put on with _____ marionettes!
4. Either Nancy or Rosa will be playing _____ guitar.
5. Stan and Ed are working on _____ animation of a snowball's life.
6. Arthur and Enid are practicing _____ lines now.
7. Have you asked Mr. Jackson or his son to contribute _____ skills?
8. Each member of the committee must do ____ part to make the pageant a success.
9. Neither Mr. Colter nor Mrs. Farrell had ____ laptop.
10. Both boys and girls must master the obstacle course to win _____ badge.

Name _______________________________ Date _______________________________

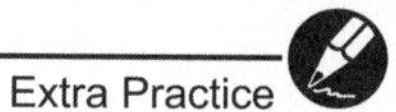

Pronouns in Comparisons

Pronouns in Comparisons *(pages L351–L352)* CHAPTER 11

EXERCISE A **Choose the pronoun that correctly completes the sentence.**

____ **1.** Greg spends more time with them than with _____.
A I
B me

____ **2.** Do you think I'm as tall as _____?
A he
B him

____ **3.** Our teacher didn't review the test with us as much as with _____.
A they
B them

____ **4.** Is Toby as old as _____?
A she
B her

____ **5.** I studied longer than _____.
A they
B them

____ **6.** The tennis tournament seemed more exciting to them than to _____.
A we
B us

____ **7.** Helmut lifts as many weights as _____.
A he
B him

____ **8.** I think Marvin is a better singer than _____.
A she
B her

____ **9.** Our cat means more to Shelby than to _____.
A I
B me

____ **10.** Hayes likes hot weather as much as _____.
A they
B them

____ **11.** Everyone should be as cheerful as _____.
A he
B him

____ **12.** Did you collect as many old newspapers as _____?
A they
B them

____ **13.** I think Robin can run faster than _____.
A I
B me

____ **14.** The people from the television station talked longer to us than to _____.
A they
B them

____ **15.** At the school crafts fair last week, no one worked harder than _____.
A we
B us

____ **16.** This chef is more experienced than _____.
A her
B she

____ **17.** I usually spend less time doing homework than _____.
A he
B him

____ **18.** I admitted that he was a better golfer than _____.
A me
B I

____ **19.** We were more interested in the exhibit than _____.
A they
B them

Student Guide
Lesson 4: Indefinite Pronoun Antecedents and Antecedent Problems

Imagine that you are with a few friends, and one is telling a joke. Everyone is smiling and waiting for the punch line. Finally, with a wink, your friend delivers the punch line, and everyone except you laughs. Your mind races as your eyes dart from face to face looking for a clue. Was it a pun? A political reference? You don't know; you just don't get it.

The way you would feel at that moment is a lot like the way a person reading an essay with unclear, missing, or confusing antecedents feels. The person cannot get the message because something very important is missing, and it's not very funny.

Lesson Objectives

- Distinguish between sentences with clear and unclear, missing, or confusing antecedents.
- Use pronouns that agree with indefinite pronoun antecedents.

PREPARE

Approximate lesson time is 25 minutes.

Materials

For the Student

BK English Language Handbook, Level I - pages L357-L365

Optional

Extra Practice Answers

BK English Language Handbook, Level I - page L365

Keywords and Pronunciation

antecedent (an-tuh-SEE-duhnt) : a word or group of words that a pronoun replaces, or refers to

indefinite pronoun : a pronoun that usually refers to unnamed people or things

---

LEARN

Activity 1: Indefinite Pronoun Antecedents and Antecedent Problems *(Offline)*

Instructions

A. Indefinite Pronouns as Antecedents

Read about using indefinite pronouns as antecedents on pages L357-L358. Then do Check Your Understanding on page L359 and Connect to the Writing Process on page L359.

Note – For Connect to the Writing Process, you need only write the word to be corrected and the correct pronoun, not the entire sentence.

B. Unclear, Missing, or Confusing Antecedents

Read about unclear, missing, or confusing antecedents on pages L362-L363. Then do Check Your Understanding on pages L363-L364, items 1-10, and Connect to the Writing Process on page L364.

C. Check Your Work

When you have finished, ask an adult to check your answers to these exercises.

D. Assessment

Go online to take the assessment.

ASSESS

Lesson Checkpoint: Indefinite Pronoun Antecedents and Antecedent Problems (*Online*)

It's time to check what you have learned. Go to the next screen to test your skills.

LEARN

Activity 2. Optional: Indefinite Pronoun Antecedents and Antecedent Problems

(Online)

Student Guide
Lesson 5: Review

In this lesson, you will answer some review questions on what you learned in this unit about using pronouns. Before you take the Unit Assessment, this is your chance to find out what you do and don't know about pronoun case; *who* and *whom* in questions and clauses; comparisons; pronouns and antecedents; indefinite pronouns; and unclear, missing, or confusing antecedents.

Lesson Objectives

- Distinguish between possessive pronouns and contractions.
- Distinguish between sentences with clear and unclear, missing, or confusing antecedents.
- Identify the use of pronouns in sentences.
- Use pronouns that agree with their antecedents in sentences.
- Use the correct pronouns to complete sentences.

PREPARE

Approximate lesson time is 25 minutes.

Materials

For the Student

BK English Language Handbook, Level I - pages L366-L367

Optional

Extra Practice Answers

BK English Language Handbook, Level I - pages L370-L371

Keywords and Pronunciation

adjective clause : a subordinate clause that is used to modify a noun or pronoun
antecedent (an-tuh-SEE-duhnt) : a word or group of words that a pronoun replaces, or refers to
case : a form of a noun or a pronoun that indicates its use in a sentence; in English there are three cases: the nominative case, the objective case, and the possessive case
clause : a group of words that has a subject and a verb
comparison : a group of words that describes similarities or differences between two or more people or things
contraction : the shortened form of two or more words, with an apostrophe to replace missing letters
elliptical clause : a subordinate clause in which words are omitted but understood to be there
gender : classification according to sex: masculine, feminine, or neuter (neither)
indefinite pronoun : a pronoun that usually refers to unnamed people or things
nominative case : noun or pronoun forms used for subjects and predicate nominatives
noun clause : a subordinate clause that is used as a noun
number : classification of a word as singular (one) or plural (more than one)
objective case : the noun or pronoun forms used for direct objects, indirect objects, or objects of prepositions
possessive case : noun or pronoun forms used to show ownership or possession
pronoun : a word that takes the place of one or more nouns

LEARN

Activity 1: Using Pronouns *(Offline)*

Instructions

A. Review

To prepare for the Unit Assessment, complete Using Pronouns Correctly, Making Personal Pronouns Agree with Their Antecedents, and Writing Sentences in the CheckPoint exercises on pages L366-L367.

B. Check Your Work

When you have finished, have an adult check your answers. Make sure you understand the corrections for any mistakes you made. If you do that, then you should be ready for the Unit Assessment.

Activity 2. Optional: Using Pronouns *(Offline)*

Instructions

Extra Practice: Complete the Posttest exercise on pages L370-L371.

When you have finished, use the Extra Practice Answers page and check your answers.

Student Guide
Lesson 6: Assessment

Lesson Objectives

- Distinguish between possessive pronouns and contractions.
- Distinguish between sentences with clear and unclear, missing, or confusing antecedents.
- Identify the use of pronouns in sentences.
- Use pronouns that agree with their antecedents in sentences.
- Use the correct pronouns to complete sentences.

PREPARE

Approximate lesson time is 25 minutes.

ASSESS

Unit Checkpoint: Using Pronouns (*Online*)

It's time to check what you have learned. Go to the next screen to test your skills.

Student Guide
Lesson 1: Agreement of Subjects and Verbs

When you need a plumber, do you call a baker? Not unless you're fond of muffins popping out of your faucet. If you want a swimming pool built, would you call a seamstress? Not unless you want to swim in a sea of seams. Naturally, you match the task you need done to a person capable of doing that task.

Just as you match a worker to a task, you must match a subject to a verb, or you may find that you do not like the result!

Lesson Objectives

- In verb phrases, use helping verbs that agree in number with their subjects.
- Use verbs that agree in number with their subjects.

PREPARE

Approximate lesson time is 25 minutes.

Materials

For the Student

BK English Language Handbook, Level I - pages L378-L386

Optional

Extra Practice Answers

BK English Language Handbook, Level I - page L386

LEARN

Activity 1: Agreement of Subjects and Verbs *(Online)*

Activity 2: Agreement of Subjects and Verbs *(Offline)*

Instructions

A. Singular and Plural Subjects

Read about singular and plural subjects on pages L378-L379. Then do Check Your Understanding on page L379.

B. Agreement with Verb Phrases

Read about agreement with verb phrases on pages L380-L381. Then do Check Your Understanding on pages L381-L382. Next do Connect to the Writing Process on page L382.

Note – For Connect to the Writing Process on page L382, you need not write out whole sentences. Just write the corrected verb form.

C. Agreement and Interrupting Words

Read about agreement and interrupting words on pages L382-L383. Then do Check Your Understanding on pages L383-L384 and Connect to the Writing Process on pages L384-L385.

D. Check Your Work

When you have finished, ask an adult to check your answers to these exercises.

E. Assessment

Go online to take the assessment.

ASSESS

Lesson Checkpoint: Agreement of Subjects and Verbs (*Online*)

It's time to check what you have learned. Go to the next screen to test your skills.

LEARN

Activity 3. Optional: Agreement of Subjects and Verbs *(Online)*

Student Guide
Lesson 2: Common Agreement Problems

When you go to a party, the guest of honor is sometimes there when you arrive. However, if the party is a surprise, the guest of honor is usually the last to arrive. Whether the guest of honor is there before everyone else, arrives after half the guests, or is last to appear, everyone agrees that he or she is still the guest of honor.

Subjects and verbs are like the guest of honor. Whether they appear early in the sentence or at the end, they are the most important words in the sentence. If you want your sentence to make sense, subjects and verbs must agree.

Lesson Objectives

- Use verbs that agree in number with compound subjects.
- Use verbs that agree in number with indefinite pronoun subjects.
- Use verbs that agree in number with subjects in sentences with inverted order.

PREPARE

Approximate lesson time is 25 minutes.

Materials

For the Student

BK English Language Handbook, Level I - pages L387-L395

Optional

Extra Practice Answers

BK English Language Handbook, Level I - page L395

Keywords and Pronunciation

compound subject : two or more subjects connected by *and* or *or* that have the same verb

inverted sentence order : sentence order in which the verb or part of the verb phrase appears before the subject

---

LEARN

Activity 1: Common Agreement Problems *(Offline)*

Instructions

A. Compound Subjects

Read about compound subjects on pages L387-L388. Then do Check Your Understanding on pages L389-L390 and Connect to the Writing Process on page L390.

B. Indefinite Pronouns as Subjects

Read about indefinite pronouns as subjects on page L391. Then do Check Your Understanding on page L392.

C. Subjects in Inverted Order

Read about subjects in inverted order on pages L392-L393. Then do Check Your Understanding on pages L393-L394.

D. Check Your Work

When you have finished, ask an adult to check your answers to these exercises.

E. Assessment

Go online to take the assessment.

ASSESS

Lesson Checkpoint: Common Agreement Problems (*Online*)

It's time to check what you have learned. Go to the next screen to test your skills.

LEARN

Activity 2. Optional: Common Agreement Problems *(Online)*

Student Guide
Lesson 3: Other Agreement Problems

In a dream, you are going to be in a wedding. You head to Joe's Formal Wear Shop for a tuxedo. Joe's motto is "Why pay more when you can get less?" Joe insists that you slip on the gray and white striped trousers. You protest that they do not go well with the gold jacket, but then Joe demands you put on plaid shoes!

Your dream becomes a nightmare as you find yourself at a luxurious wedding reception. People are dancing; the music stops, and all eyes are glued on you!

If you wear clothes that don't match the occasion, you'll feel embarrassed. If you use subjects and verbs that don't agree, the result will be pretty much the same.

Lesson Objectives

- Use contractions whose verb parts agree in number with their subjects.
- Use verbs that agree in number with collective noun subjects.
- Use verbs that agree in number with subjects that express amounts.
- Use verbs that agree in number with their subjects.

PREPARE

Approximate lesson time is 25 minutes.

Materials

For the Student

BK English Language Handbook, Level I - pages L396-L403

Optional

Extra Practice Answers

BK English Language Handbook, Level I - page L403

Keywords and Pronunciation

collective noun : a word that names a group of people or things

contraction : the shortened form of two or more words, with an apostrophe to replace missing letters

linking verb : a verb that links the subject with another word that renames or describes the subject

LEARN

Activity 1: Other Agreement Problems *(Offline)*

Instructions

A. *Doesn't* or *Don't*, Collective Nouns, Words Expressing Amounts

Read about subject and verb agreement when using *doesn't* or *don't*, collective nouns, and words expressing amounts on pages L396-L397. Then do Check Your Understanding on page L398.

B. Singular Nouns That Have Plural Forms, Subjects with Linking Verbs, Titles

Read about subject and verb agreement when using singular nouns that have plural forms, subjects with linking verbs, and titles on pages L399-L400. Then do Check Your Understanding on pages L400-L401 and Connect to the Writing Process on page L401.

C. Check Your Work

When you have finished, ask an adult to check your answers to these exercises.

D. Assessment

Go online to take the assessment.

ASSESS

Lesson Checkpoint: Other Agreement Problems (*Online*)

It's time to check what you have learned. Go to the next screen to test your skills.

LEARN

Activity 2. Optional: Other Agreement Problems *(Online)*

Student Guide

Lesson 4: Review

In this lesson, you will answer some review questions on what you learned in this unit about subject and verb agreement. Before you take the Unit Assessment, this is your chance to find out what you do and don't know about making subjects and verbs agree in sentences with singular and plural subjects, with compound subjects, with indefinite pronouns as subjects, with collective nouns as subjects, and with other kinds of words as subjects.

Lesson Objectives

- Use verbs that agree in number with their subjects.

PREPARE

Approximate lesson time is 25 minutes.

Materials

For the Student

BK English Language Handbook, Level I - pages L404-L405

Optional

Extra Practice Answers

BK English Language Handbook, Level I - pages L408-L409

Keywords and Pronunciation

agreement of subject and verb : when a subject and verb match in number

collective noun : a word that names a group of people or things

compound subject : two or more subjects connected by *and* or *or* that have the same verb

indefinite pronoun : a pronoun that usually refers to unnamed people or things

number : classification of a word as singular (one) or plural (more than one)

LEARN

Activity 1: Subject and Verb Agreement *(Offline)*

Instructions

A. Review

To prepare for the Unit Assessment, complete Making Subjects and Verbs Agree, Subject and Verb Agreement, and Writing Sentences in the CheckPoint exercises on pages L404-L405.

B. Check Your Work

When you have finished, have an adult check your answers. Make sure you understand the corrections for any mistakes you made. If you do that, then you should be ready for the Unit Assessment.

Activity 2. Optional: Subject and Verb Agreement *(Offline)*

Instructions

Extra Practice: Complete the Posttest exercise on pages L408-L409.

When you have finished, use the Extra Practice Answers page and check your answers.

Student Guide
Lesson 5: Assessment

Lesson Objectives

- Use verbs that agree in number with their subjects.

PREPARE

Approximate lesson time is 25 minutes.

ASSESS

Unit Checkpoint: Subject and Verb Agreement (*Online*)

It's time to check what you have learned. Go to the next screen to test your skills.

Student Guide
Lesson 1: Comparison of Adjectives and Adverbs

Picture this: You have been training with swim teams for eight years. Sidestroke, breaststroke, backstroke—you excel at all of them. The statewide championship was last night. You won!

This morning you ripped open the sports section, and the article about the swim meet said some other kid was the best swimmer and that you came in third!

Good, better, best—do the degrees of comparison really matter? They do to you!

Lesson Objectives

- Identify logical and illogical comparisons.
- Use good and well correctly in sentences.
- Use negative words correctly in sentences.
- Use other and else correctly in comparisons.
- Use the correct form of comparison of adjectives and adverbs in sentences.
- Use good and well correctly in sentences.
- Use other and else correctly in comparisons.

PREPARE

Approximate lesson time is 25 minutes.

Materials

For the Student

BK English Language Handbook, Level I - pages L413-L429

Optional

Extra Practice Answers

BK English Language Handbook, Level I - pages L426 and L429

Keywords and Pronunciation

adjective : a word that modifies, or describes, a noun or pronoun

adverb : a word that modifies a verb, an adjective, or another adverb

comparative degree of comparison : describes by comparing two persons, places, things, or actions

degree of comparison : the way in which adjectives and adverbs describe by comparing persons, places, things, or actions; the three degrees of comparison are positive, comparative, and superlative

double comparison : the error of using two methods of comparison simultaneously

illogical comparison : an incomplete comparison in which two different things are compared

modifier : a word or phrase that describes or changes another word's or phrase's meaning

positive degree of comparison : describes persons, places, things, or actions without comparing

superlative degree of comparison : describes by comparing more than two persons, places, things, or actions

LEARN

Activity 1: Comparison of Adjectives and Adverbs *(Online)*

Activity 2: Comparison of Adjectives and Adverbs *(Offline)*

Instructions

A. Regular and Irregular Comparison

Read about regular and irregular comparison on pages L413-L421. Then do Check Your Understanding on page L417, items 1-10. Next do QuickCheck on page L421.

B. Double Comparisons, Illogical Comparisons, Other and Else in Comparisons

Read about double comparisons, illogical comparisons, and *other* and *else* in comparisons on pages L422-L423. Then do Check Your Understanding and Connect to the Writing Process on page L424.

C. Problems with Modifiers

Read about other problems with modifiers on pages L427-L428. Then do Check Your Understanding on page L428. Next do Connect to the Writing Process on the same page.

Note – For the Connect to the Writing Process on page L428, you need only write the corrections. Writing the entire sentence is not necessary.

D. Check Your Work

When you have finished, ask an adult to check your answers to these exercises.

E. Assessment

Go online to take the assessment.

ASSESS

Lesson Checkpoint: Comparison of Adjectives and Adverbs (*Online*)

It's time to check what you have learned. Go to the next screen to test your skills.

LEARN

Activity 3: Comparison of Adjectives and Adverbs *(Online)*

Student Guide
Lesson 2: Review

In this lesson, you will answer some review questions on what you learned in this unit about using adjectives and adverbs. Before you take the Unit Assessment, this is your chance to find out what you do and don't know about regular and irregular comparisons, double comparisons, illogical comparisons, *other* and *else* in comparisons, and other problems with modifiers.

Lesson Objectives

- Identify logical and illogical comparisons.
- Use negative words correctly in sentences.
- Use the correct form of adjectives and adverbs in sentences.

PREPARE

Approximate lesson time is 25 minutes.

Materials

For the Student

BK English Language Handbook, Level I - pages L430-L431

Optional

Extra Practice Answers

BK English Language Handbook, Level I - pages L434-L435

Keywords and Pronunciation

double comparison : the error of using two methods of comparison simultaneously
illogical comparison : an incomplete comparison in which two different things are compared
modifier : a word or phrase that describes or changes another word's or phrase's meaning

---

LEARN

Activity 1: Using Adjectives and Adverbs *(Offline)*

Instructions

A. Review

To prepare for the Unit Assessment, complete Using Modifiers Correctly on page L430 and Writing with Modifiers on page L431 in the CheckPoint exercises on pages L430-L431.

Note – For both CheckPoint exercises, you need only write the corrections needed. Writing the entire sentence is not necessary.

B. Check Your Work

When you have finished, have an adult check your answers. Make sure you understand the corrections for any mistakes you made. If you do that, then you should be ready for the Unit Assessment.

Activity 2: Using Adjectives and Adverbs *(Offline)*

Instructions

Extra Practice: Complete the Posttest exercise on pages L434-L435.

Student Guide
Lesson 3: Assessment

Lesson Objectives

- Identify logical and illogical comparisons.
- Use negative words correctly in sentences.
- Use the correct form of adjectives and adverbs in sentences.

PREPARE

Approximate lesson time is 25 minutes.

ASSESS

Unit Checkpoint: Using Adjectives and Adverbs (*Online*)

It's time to check what you have learned. Go to the next screen to test your skills.

Student Guide
Lesson 1: Capitalization

"No shoes, no shirt, no service." That's what the sign says on restaurant doors all over the country. Even on the beach, if you want to enter these places, you must meet these minimum requirements. In town, you may find that the requirements are increased. Some restaurants require a tie for men; others require a jacket. The more formal the establishment, the more requirements.

Writing also has minimum requirements so that others can easily read what is written. Without shoes, you will not be served in many places. Without capital letters, your writing will not be read by many people.

Lesson Objectives

- Capitalize proper nouns and their abbreviations.
- Capitalize the first word of the greeting and the closing of a letter.
- Capitalize the parts of an outline correctly.

PREPARE

Approximate lesson time is 25 minutes.

Materials

For the Student

BK English Language Handbook, Level I - pages L459-L476

Extra Practice Answers

Optional

BK English Language Handbook, Level I - pages L478-L479

Keywords and Pronunciation

proper noun : the name of a particular person, place, thing, or idea; capitalized

---

LEARN

Activity 1: Capitalization *(Online)*

Activity 2: Capitalization *(Offline)*

Instructions

A. Capitalization Review

Read about capitalization on pages L459-L479. Then do Check Your Understanding on page L462. Next do the two Check Your Understanding exercises on pages L465-L467, pages L469-L471, and pages L475-L476.

B. Check Your Work

When you have finished, ask an adult to check your answers to these exercises.

C. Assessment

Go online to take the assessment.

ASSESS

Lesson Checkpoint: Capitalization (*Online*)

It's time to check what you have learned. Go to the next screen to test your skills.

LEARN

Activity 3: Capitalization *(Online)*

Student Guide
Lesson 2: More Capitalization

If you want the best of everything, you'll need to travel the world. Each country has at least one thing for which it is justly famous. For instance, many women all over the globe clamor for Italy's shoes. The accuracy of Switzerland's watches is well known. And who within earshot of a radio can't name the land of rock and roll?

Like a brand, the country's name precedes the specialty: Irish lace, French cooking, and Caribbean beaches. The capital letters for each of these proper adjectives carry a lot of pride. Be respectful; capitalize proper adjectives.

Lesson Objectives

- Capitalize a person's title when it is used instead of a name or for direct address.
- Capitalize a person's title when it precedes a name.
- Capitalize important words in the titles of written works and other works of art.
- Capitalize proper adjectives.

PREPARE

Approximate lesson time is 25 minutes.

Materials

For the Student

BK English Language Handbook, Level I - pages L479-L486

Extra Practice Answers

Optional

BK English Language Handbook, Level I - pages L486-L487

Keywords and Pronunciation

article : a kind of adjective; the articles are a, an, and the

conjunction : a word that connects words or groups of words

preposition : a word that shows the relationship between a noun or a pronoun and another word in the sentence

proper adjective : an adjective form of a proper noun; for example, *European* or *Japanese*

LEARN

Activity 1: More Capitalization *(Offline)*

Instructions

A. Proper Adjectives

Read about capitalizing proper adjectives on pages L479-L480. Then do Check Your Understanding on page L480. Next do Connect to the Writing Process on page L480.

Note – For Connect to the Writing Process on page L480, you need not write the entire paragraph. Just write the words that should be capitalized.

B. Titles

Read about capitalizing titles on pages L481-L482. Then do Check Your Understanding on pages L482-L483. Next do Connect to the Writing Process on page L483.

Note – For Connect to the Writing Process on page L483, you need not write the entire paragraph. Just write the words that should be capitalized.

C. Titles of Written Works and Other Works of Art

Read about capitalizing titles of written works and other works of art on pages L483-L484. Then do Check Your Understanding on pages L484-L485 and Connect to the Writing Process on pages L485-L486.
Note – For Connect to the Writing Process on pages L485-L486, you need not write the entire paragraph. Just write the words that should be capitalized.

Note – Although the book states that a preposition should not be capitalized unless it is the first word in a title, prepositions in titles are usually capitalized if they contain five or more letters.

D. Check Your Work

When you have finished, ask an adult to check your answers to these exercises.

E. Assessment

Go online to take the assessment.

ASSESS

Lesson Checkpoint: More Capitalization (*Online*)

It's time to check what you have learned. Go to the next screen to test your skills.

LEARN

Activity 2: More Capitalization *(Online)*

Student Guide
Lesson 3: Review

In this lesson, you will answer some review questions on what you learned in this unit about capital letters. Before you take the Unit Assessment, this is your chance to find out what you do and don't know about capitalizing the first word in sentences, parts of letters, the pronoun *I*, proper nouns, proper adjectives, and titles.

Lesson Objectives

- Recognize and use correct capitalization.

PREPARE

Approximate lesson time is 25 minutes.

Materials

For the Student

BK English Language Handbook, Level I - pages L488-L489

Extra Practice Answers

Keywords and Pronunciation

article : a kind of adjective; the articles are a, an, and the
conjunction : a word that connects words or groups of words
preposition : a word that shows the relationship between a noun or a pronoun and another word in the sentence
proper adjective : an adjective form of a proper noun; for example, *European* or *Japanese*
proper noun : the name of a particular person, place, thing, or idea; capitalized

---

LEARN

Activity 1: Capital Letters *(Offline)*

Instructions

A. Review

To prepare for the Unit Assessment, complete Using Capital Letters Correctly on page L488 and Editing for the Correct Use of Capital Letters in the CheckPoint exercises on pages L488-L489.

B. Check Your Work

When you have finished, have an adult check your answers. Make sure you understand the corrections for any mistakes you made. If you do that, then you should be ready for the Unit Assessment.

Activity 2: Capital Letters *(Offline)*

Instructions

Extra Practice: Complete the Posttest exercise on pages L492-L493.

When you have finished, use the Extra Practice Answers page and check your answers.

Student Guide
Lesson 4: Assessment

Lesson Objectives

- Recognize and use correct capitalization.

PREPARE

Approximate lesson time is 25 minutes.

ASSESS

Unit Checkpoint: Capital Letters (*Online*)

It's time to check what you have learned. Go to the next screen to test your skills.

Student Guide
Lesson 1: End Marks

Imagine a new kind of newspaper! This newspaper will have no headlines. Each story will be printed one right after the other with no breaks between them. Lots of money and tons of paper will be saved! What do you think?

What? You don't like the idea! You think the newspaper will be hard to read and take up too much time? Well, maybe you're right. Just as headlines tell readers where a story starts, end marks—such as periods, question marks, and exclamation points—tell readers where a thought ends. Without end marks, readers don't know whether an idea is coming or going!

Lesson Objectives

- Use a period, question mark, or exclamation point at the end of sentences.
- Use periods correctly in abbreviations and outlines.

PREPARE

Approximate lesson time is 25 minutes.

Materials

For the Student

BK English Language Handbook, Level I - pages L497-L503

Optional

Extra Practice Answers

BK English Language Handbook, Level I - page L504

Keywords and Pronunciation

clause : a group of words that has a subject and a verb
compound sentence : two or more simple sentences, joined by a comma and coordinating conjunction or by a semicolon
declarative sentence : a sentence that makes a statement or expresses an opinion and ends with a period
end mark : the punctuation mark at the end of a sentence
exclamatory sentence : a sentence that expresses strong feeling or emotion and ends with an exclamation point
imperative sentence : a sentence that gives a direction, makes a request, or gives a command; it ends with either a period or an exclamation point
interrogative sentence : a sentence that asks a question and ends with a question mark

LEARN

Activity 1: End Marks *(Online)*

Activity 2: End Marks *(Offline)*

Instructions

A. End Marks

Read about end marks on pages L497-L499. Then do Check Your Understanding on page L499. Next, do Connect to the Writing Process on pages L499-L500.

B. Other Uses of the Period

Read about other uses of the period on pages L500-L502. Then do Check Your Understanding on page L503. Next, do Connect to the Writing Process on the same page.

C. Check Your Work

When you have finished, ask an adult to check your answers to these exercises.

D. Assessment

Go online to take the assessment.

ASSESS

Lesson Checkpoint: End Marks (*Online*)

It's time to check what you have learned. Go to the next screen to test your skills.

LEARN

Activity 3. Optional: End Marks *(Online)*

Student Guide
Lesson 2: Commas That Separate

Here's an idea to save money on house construction. Instead of building a lot of little rooms, just build one big room! Not only will these new houses save money, but they will help families stay in touch since everyone will be together all the time. What do you think?

You don't care for this idea? You want to keep your things separate from your brothers' and sisters' stuff! Oh, well, perhaps you're right. Just as a house needs rooms to keep everything in its place, sentences need commas to separate words, phrases, and clauses so that sentences are understandable.

Lesson Objectives

- Use commas after certain introductory elements.
- Use commas before the coordinating conjunctions that join the parts of compound sentences.
- Use commas correctly with dates and addresses and in letters.
- Use commas to separate certain adjectives before nouns.
- Use commas to separate items in a series.

PREPARE

Approximate lesson time is 25 minutes.

Materials

For the Student

BK English Language Handbook, Level I - pages L505-L518

Optional

Extra Practice Answers

BK English Language Handbook, Level I - pages L519-L520

Keywords and Pronunciation

adjective : a word that modifies, or describes, a noun or pronoun

adverb clause : a subordinate clause that is used mainly to modify a verb

compound sentence : two or more simple sentences, joined by a comma and coordinating conjunction or by a semicolon

participial phrase : a participle joined with related words

prepositional phrase : a group of words that begins with a preposition, ends with a noun or pronoun, and is used as an adjective or adverb

LEARN

Activity 1: Commas That Separate *(Offline)*

Instructions

A. Items in a Series

Read about commas that separate items in a series on pages L505-L506. Then do Check Your Understanding on page L506.

B. Adjectives Before Nouns

Read about using commas to separate adjectives that come before nouns on page L508. Then do Check Your Understanding and Connect to the Writing Process: Editing on page L509.

Note – For all of the Connect to the Writing Process exercises assigned in this lesson, you need not write entire sentences. Just write the words that appear before the comma and add the comma.

C. Compound Sentences

Read about using commas to separate the clauses in a compound sentence on pages L510-L511. Then do Check Your Understanding on pages L511-L512 and Connect to the Writing Process: Editing on page L512.

D. Introductory Elements

Read about using commas after introductory elements on pages L513-L514. Then do Check Your Understanding on pages L514-L515 and Connect to the Writing Process: Editing on page L515.

E. Commonly Used Commas

Read about commas with dates and addresses and in letters on pages L515-L517. Then do Check Your Understanding on pages L517-L518.

F. Check Your Work

When you have finished, ask an adult to check your answers to these exercises.

G. Assessment

Go online to take the assessment.

ASSESS

Lesson Checkpoint: Commas That Separate (*Online*)

It's time to check what you have learned. Go to the next screen to test your skills.

LEARN

Activity 2. Optional: Commas That Separate *(Online)*

Student Guide
Lesson 3: Commas That Enclose

What kind of a comma person are you? Some people seem to not like commas at all. Their writing hardly ever contains a comma. Other people seem to love commas. They put in commas whether or not there is a good reason for using them.

This lesson will give you more reasons to use commas—or not.

Lesson Objectives

- Use commas to enclose nouns of direct address.
- Use commas to enclose parenthetical expressions.
- Use commas to set off appositives in sentences.
- Use commas to set off nonessential participial phrases and nonessential clauses in sentences.

PREPARE

Approximate lesson time is 25 minutes.

Materials

For the Student

BK English Language Handbook, Level I - pages L521-L532

Optional

Extra Practice Answers

BK English Language Handbook, Level I - pages L528, L533

Keywords and Pronunciation

appositive : a noun or pronoun that identifies or explains another noun or pronoun in the sentence
clause : a group of words that has a subject and a verb
direct address : calling a person or animal by name or title; for example, "Look, Mary," or "Doctor, come"
essential element : a word or a group of words that is necessary to a sentence's meaning
nonessential element : an interrupting word or group of words that is not necessary to the meaning of a sentence
parenthetical expression : a word or words that interrupt a sentence; for example, *I believe, of course*
participial phrase : a participle joined with related words

LEARN

Activity 1: Commas That Enclose *(Offline)*

Instructions

A. Direct Address

Read about commas that enclose nouns of direct address on page L521. Then do Check Your Understanding and Connect to the Writing Process: Editing on page L522.

Note –For all of the Connect to the Writing Process exercises assigned in this lesson, you need not write entire sentences. Just write the words that should be followed by commas and add the commas.

B. Parenthetical Expressions

Read about using commas to enclose parenthetical expressions on pages L523-L524. Then do Check Your Understanding and Connect to the Writing Process: Editing on pages L524-L525.

C. Appositives

Read about when to use commas to enclose appositives and when not to use them on pages L525-L526. Then do Check Your Understanding and Connect to the Writing Process: Editing on page L527.

D. Nonessential and Essential Elements

Read about the difference between nonessential and essential elements and when to use commas on pages L529-L530. Then do Check Your Understanding and Connect to the Writing Process: Editing on pages L530-L531.

E. Check Your Work

When you have finished, ask an adult to check your answers to these exercises.

F. Assessment

Go online to take the assessment.

ASSESS

Lesson Assessment: Commas That Enclose (*Online*)

Follow the directions to take this assessment online.

LEARN

Activity 2. Optional: Commas That Enclose *(Offline)*

Student Guide
Lesson 4: Review

In this lesson, you will answer some review questions on what you learned in this unit about end marks and commas. Before you take the Unit Assessment, this is your chance to find out what you do and don't know about punctuating sentences, abbreviations, outlines, items in a series, adjectives, introductory elements, dates, addresses, letters, nouns of direct address, parenthetical expressions, appositives, and nonessential elements.

Lesson Objectives

- Use end marks and commas correctly.

PREPARE

Approximate lesson time is 25 minutes.

Materials

For the Student

BK English Language Handbook, Level I - pages L534-L535

Optional

Extra Practice Answers

BK English Language Handbook, Level I - pages L538-L539

Keywords and Pronunciation

adjective : a word that modifies, or describes, a noun or pronoun

adverb clause : a subordinate clause that is used mainly to modify a verb

appositive : a noun or pronoun that identifies or explains another noun or pronoun in the sentence

clause : a group of words that has a subject and a verb

compound sentence : two or more simple sentences, joined by a comma and coordinating conjunction or by a semicolon

declarative sentence : a sentence that makes a statement or expresses an opinion and ends with a period

direct address : calling a person or animal by name or title; for example, "Look, Mary," or "Doctor, come"

essential element : a word or a group of words that is necessary to a sentence's meaning

exclamatory sentence : a sentence that expresses strong feeling or emotion and ends with an exclamation point

imperative sentence : a sentence that gives a direction, makes a request, or gives a command; it ends with either a period or an exclamation point

interrogative sentence : a sentence that asks a question and ends with a question mark

nonessential element : an interrupting word or group of words that is not necessary to the meaning of a sentence

parenthetical expression : a word or words that interrupt a sentence; for example, *I believe, of course*

participial phrase : a participle joined with related words

prepositional phrase : a group of words that begins with a preposition, ends with a noun or pronoun, and is used as an adjective or adverb

LEARN

Activity 1: End Marks and Commas *(Offline)*

Instructions

A. Review

To prepare for the Unit Assessment, complete Understanding Kinds of Sentences and End Marks, Using Commas Correctly, and Writing Sentences in the CheckPoint exercises on pages L534-L535.

Note – For the CheckPoint exercises, you need not write entire sentences. Instead, just write the words that should be followed by a punctuation mark and add the appropriate mark.

B. Check Your Work

When you have finished, have an adult check your answers. Make sure you understand the corrections for any mistakes you made. If you do that, then you should be ready for the Unit Assessment.

Activity 2. Optional: End Marks and Commas *(Offline)*

Instructions

Extra Practice: Complete the Posttest exercise on pages L538-L539.

When you have finished, use the Extra Practice Answers page to check your answers.

Student Guide
Lesson 5: Assessment

Lesson Objectives

- Use end marks and commas correctly.

PREPARE

Approximate lesson time is 25 minutes.

ASSESS

Unit Checkpoint: End Marks and Commas (*Online*)

It's time to check what you have learned. Go to the next screen to test your skills.

Student Guide
Lesson 1: Uses of Italics and Quotation Marks

For special occasions, people wear special clothes. For example, at a wedding anywhere in the world, you can usually identify the bride. Her dress is different from that of other women, and people treat her differently. You can even recognize her bridesmaids because they are often dressed alike in some way. Their dresses show that they belong together.

Titles are like the women in a bridal party. Instead of all dressing in similar clothes, titles are printed in all italics or are enclosed in quotation marks.

Lesson Objectives

- Italicize or underline letters, numbers, and words used to represent themselves.
- Italicize or underline the names of airplanes, ships, trains, and spacecrafts.
- Italicize or underline the titles of long written or musical works.
- Italicize or underline the titles of paintings and sculptures.
- Use quotation marks to enclose the titles of chapters, articles, stories, one-act plays, most poems, and songs.
- Use quotation marks to enclose the titles of chapters, articles, short stories, most poems, and songs.

PREPARE

Approximate lesson time is 25 minutes.

Materials

For the Student

BK English Language Handbook, Level I - pages L543-L549

Optional

Extra Practice Answers

BK English Language Handbook, Level I - pages L550-L551

LEARN

Activity 1: Uses of Italics and Quotation Marks *(Online)*

Activity 2: Uses of Italics and Quotation Marks *(Offline)*

Instructions

A. Italics

Read about using italics (underlining) on pages L543-L545. Then do Check Your Understanding on pages L545-L546 and Connect to the Writing Process: Editing on pages L546-L547.

Note –For Connect to the Writing Process: Editing on pages L546-L547, you need not write out entire sentences. Just write the words that require underlining.

B. Quotation Marks for Titles

Read about using quotation marks for titles on page L548. Then do Check Your Understanding and Connect to the Writing Process: Drafting on page L549.

C. Check Your Work

When you have finished, ask an adult to check your answers to these exercises.

D. Assessment

Go online to take the assessment.

ASSESS

Lesson Checkpoint: Uses of Italics and Quotation Marks (*Online*)

It's time to check what you have learned. Go to the next screen to test your skills.

LEARN

Activity 3. Optional: Uses of Italics and Quotation Marks *(Online)*

Student Guide
Lesson 2: Direct Quotations

Here's an example of a common situation. Carlos plays a song he wrote for you and some other friends. That night, you tell Joe that you think Carlos's song needs a better title. Two days later Carlos comes up to you and says, "Hey! I hear that you think my song is rotten!"

Times like these call for quotation marks. Quotation marks enclose a person's exact words. The difference between a direct quotation of yours and someone's indirect quotation of your words can be a friendship lost.

Lesson Objectives

- Capitalize direct quotations correctly.
- Distinguish between direct and indirect quotations.
- Use commas and end marks correctly in direct quotations.
- Use quotation marks correctly in direct quotations.
- Punctuate quotations correctly.

PREPARE

Approximate lesson time is 25 minutes.

Materials

For the Student

BK English Language Handbook, Level I - pages L551-L558

Optional

Extra Practice Answers

BK English Language Handbook, Level I - pages L559-L560

Keywords and Pronunciation

direct quotation : the exact words of a speaker or writer

end mark : the punctuation mark at the end of a sentence

indirect quotation : repeating the idea of someone else, without using the exact words; indirect quotations do not use quotation marks, are punctuated like regular sentences, and are often introduced by the word *that*

LEARN

Activity 1: Direct Quotations *(Offline)*

Instructions

A. Quotation Marks with Direct Quotations

Read about using quotation marks with direct quotations on pages L551-L553. Then do Check Your Understanding and Connect to the Writing Process: Editing on page L553.

B. Capital Letters with Direct Quotations

Read about using capital letters with direct quotations on pages L553-L554. Then do Check Your Understanding and Connect to the Writing Process: Editing on page L554.

Note – For Connect to the Writing Process on page L554, you need not write entire sentences. Just write the word that should be either capitalized or lowercased.

C. Commas with Direct Quotations

Read about using commas with direct quotations on page L555. Then complete Check Your Understanding on pages L555-L556 and Connect to the Writing Process: Editing on page L556.

D. End Marks with Direct Quotations

Read about using end marks with direct quotations on pages L556-L557. Then do Check Your Understanding on pages L557-L558 and Connect to the Writing Process: Editing on page L558.

E. Check Your Work

When you have finished, ask an adult to check your answers to these exercises.

F. Assessment

Go online to take the assessment.

ASSESS

Lesson Checkpoint: Direct Quotations (*Online*)

It's time to check what you have learned. Go to the next screen to test your skills.

LEARN

Activity 2. Optional: Direct Quotations *(Online)*

Student Guide
Lesson 3: Other Uses of Quotation Marks

In the "olden days," a gentleman always opened the door for a lady and held it while the lady entered. Most people in the United States agreed on this rule. Some still do. The convention was useful because it prevented crowding at doors and allowed people to enter and exit without confusion or accident.

The rules of punctuating dialogue are like the rules of etiquette. They prevent confusion because they help people to understand what is happening and to anticipate what is going to happen. When you write and quote dialogue, follow the rules, or you may find a door slammed in your face!

Lesson Objectives

- Paragraph dialogue correctly.
- Punctuate and capitalize dialogue correctly.
- Use quotation marks correctly with long passages.
- Use single quotation marks correctly.

PREPARE

Approximate lesson time is 25 minutes.

Materials

For the Student

BK English Language Handbook, Level I - pages L560-L564

Optional

Extra Practice Answers

BK English Language Handbook, Level I - page L565

Keywords and Pronunciation

dialogue : a conversation between characters

LEARN

Activity 1: Other Uses of Quotation Marks *(Offline)*

Instructions

A. Dialogue, Long Passages, Quotations Within Quotations

Read about punctuating dialogue, long passages, and quotations within quotations on pages L560-L561. Then do Check Your Understanding on pages L563-L564 and Connect to the Writing Process: Editing on page L564.

B. Check Your Work

When you have finished, ask an adult to check your answers to these exercises.

C. Assessment

Go online to take the assessment.

ASSESS

Lesson Assessment: Other Uses of Quotation Marks (*Online*)

Follow the directions to take this assessment online.

LEARN

Activity 2. Optional: Other Uses of Quotation Marks *(Online)*

Student Guide
Lesson 4: Review

In this lesson, you will answer some review questions on what you learned in this unit about italics and quotation marks. Before you take the Unit Assessment, this is your chance to find out what you do and don't know about using quotation marks or italics for titles; italicizing letters, numbers, and words that represent themselves; using quotation marks, commas, capitalization, and end marks with direct quotations; recognizing indirect quotations; paragraphing dialogue; and using single quotation marks.

Lesson Objectives

- Capitalize direct quotations and dialogue correctly.
- Distinguish between direct and indirect quotations.
- Paragraph dialogue correctly.
- Use commas and end marks correctly in direct quotations and dialogue.
- Use italics or underlining correctly.
- Use quotation marks correctly.
- Use single quotation marks correctly.

PREPARE

Approximate lesson time is 25 minutes.

Materials

For the Student

BK English Language Handbook, Level I - pages L566-L567

Optional

Extra Practice Answers

BK English Language Handbook, Level I - pages L570-L571

Keywords and Pronunciation

dialogue : a conversation between characters

direct quotation : the exact words of a speaker or writer

end mark : the punctuation mark at the end of a sentence

indirect quotation : repeating the idea of someone else, without using the exact words; indirect quotations do not use quotation marks, are punctuated like regular sentences, and are often introduced by the word *that*

LEARN

Activity 1: Italics and Quotation Marks *(Offline)*

Instructions

A. Review

To prepare for the Unit Assessment, complete the first Punctuating Quotations Correctly exercise and items 1-5 of the second Punctuating Quotations Correctly exercise in the CheckPoint exercises on pages L566-L567.

B. Check Your Work

When you have finished, have an adult check your answers. Make sure you understand the corrections for any mistakes you made. If you do that, then you should be ready for the Unit Assessment.

Activity 2. Optional: Italics and Quotation Marks *(Offline)*

Instructions

Extra Practice: Complete the Posttest exercise on pages L570-L571.

When you have finished, use the Extra Practice Answers page and check your answers.

Student Guide
Lesson 5: Assessment

Lesson Objectives

- Capitalize direct quotations and dialogue correctly.
- Distinguish between direct and indirect quotations.
- Paragraph dialogue correctly.
- Use commas and end marks correctly in direct quotations and dialogue.
- Use italics or underlining correctly.
- Use quotation marks correctly.
- Use single quotation marks correctly.

PREPARE

Approximate lesson time is 25 minutes.

ASSESS

Unit Checkpoint: Italics and Quotation Marks (*Online*)

It's time to check what you have learned. Go to the next screen to test your skills.

Student Guide
Lesson 1: Apostrophes

For many toddlers, one of their first words is "MINE!" When toddlers begin to grow, they like name labels. "Maggie," says the license plate on the bike. "Matt's Room!" blares the sign on the bedroom door. Finally, when the kids become adults, they monogram everything they own—even the towels.

The apostrophe is just a tiny little curly-q, but its meaning matters because when an apostrophe is combined with an *s* and follows your name, it means "MINE."

Lesson Objectives

- Distinguish between contractions and possessive pronouns.
- Use apostrophes correctly in contractions.
- Use apostrophes correctly to show joint and separate ownership.
- Use apostrophes correctly to show possession.
- Use apostrophes correctly when forming the plurals of letters, symbols, numerals, and words used as words.
- Use apostrophes correctly with certain dates.
- Use apostrophes correctly with nouns expressing time or amount.
- Use the correct possessive forms of personal and indefinite pronouns.

PREPARE

Approximate lesson time is 25 minutes.

Materials

For the Student

BK English Language Handbook, Level I - pages L575-L588

Optional

Extra Practice Answers

BK English Language Handbook, Level I - pages L584-L585, page L589

Keywords and Pronunciation

compound word : two or more words used together as a single word; may be written as one connected word, as separate words, or with hyphens between the words

indefinite pronoun : a pronoun that usually refers to unnamed people or things

personal pronoun : a pronoun that varies its form to show the person(s) speaking (first person), the person(s) spoken to (second person), or the person(s) spoken about (third person)

LEARN

Activity 1: Apostrophes *(Online)*

Activity 2: Apostrophes *(Offline)*

Instructions

A. Possession

Read about using apostrophes to indicate possession on pages L575-L580. Then do Check Your Understanding on pages L576-L577, items 1-10. Next, do the first Check Your Understanding on page L578, items 1-10. Then complete Check Your Understanding on page L580.

B. Joint and Separate Ownership, Nouns of Time and Amount

Read about using apostrophes to indicate joint and separate ownership and to indicate time and amounts on pages L581-L582. Then do Check Your Understanding on page L582 and Connect to the Writing Process: Editing on the next page.

Note – For Connect to the Writing Process: Editing on page L583, you need only write the correct possessive form.

C. Other Uses

Read about other uses of apostrophes on pages L585-L588. Then do the second Check Your Understanding exercise on pages L586-L587. Next do Check Your Understanding on page L588 and Connect to the Writing Process: Editing on the same page.

Note – For Connect to the Writing Process: Editing on page L588, you need not write entire sentences. Just correctly write the word(s) that should be revised.

D. Check Your Work

When you have finished, ask an adult to check your answers to these exercises.

E. Assessment

Go online to take the assessment.

ASSESS

Lesson Assessment: Apostrophes (*Online*)

Follow the directions to take this assessment online.

LEARN

Activity 3. Optional: Apostrophes *(Online)*

Student Guide
Lesson 2: Semicolons

"It cooks! It cleans! It darns socks! It's the Pocket Do-All!" You've heard or seen the advertisements for products that claim to serve several purposes. Like pens with two colors of ink, they can be wonderful, especially for certain jobs.

Semicolons are like the Pocket-Do-All; they are partly periods and partly commas, and they are particularly suited to certain kinds of sentences.

Lesson Objectives

- Use semicolons between clauses in compound sentences that are joined by conjunctive adverbs or transitional words.
- Use semicolons between clauses of compound sentences connected with a coordinating conjunction if there are commas within a clause.
- Use semicolons between items in a series if the items themselves contain commas.
- Use semicolons to punctuate compound sentences not joined by a conjunction.

PREPARE

Approximate lesson time is 25 minutes.

Materials

For the Student

BK English Language Handbook, Level I - pages L590-L595

Optional

Extra Practice Answers

BK English Language Handbook, Level I - page L596

Keywords and Pronunciation

clause : a group of words that has a subject and a verb
compound sentence : two or more simple sentences, joined by a comma and coordinating conjunction or by a semicolon
conjunctive adverb : adverbs, such as however, used to join independent clauses but also may be used as parenthetical expressions
independent clause : a clause that can stand alone as a sentence because it expresses a complete idea
parenthetical expression : a word or words that interrupt a sentence; for example, *I believe*, *of course*
transitional word or phrase : word or phrase, such as for example, used to move from one idea to another

LEARN

Activity 1: Semicolons *(Offline)*

Instructions

A. Semicolons with Conjunctive Adverbs

Read about using semicolons with conjunctive adverbs on pages L590-L591.Then do the two Check Your Understanding exercises on pages L592-L593 and Connect to the Writing Process: Editing on page L593.

Note – For the Connect to the Writing Process: Editing on page L593, you need not rewrite entire sentences. Just write the word preceding the needed punctuation mark and the punctuation mark.

B. Semicolons to Avoid Confusion

Read about using semicolons to avoid confusion on page L594. Then do Check Your Understanding on pages L594-L595 and Connect to the Writing Process: Editing on page L595.

Note – For the Connect to the Writing Process: Editing on page L595, you need not rewrite entire sentences. Just write the word preceding the needed punctuation mark and the punctuation mark.

C. Check Your Work

When you have finished, ask an adult to check your answers to these exercises.

D. Assessment

Go online to take the assessment.

ASSESS

Lesson Assessment: Semicolons (*Online*)

It's time to check what you have learned. Go to the next screen to test your skills.

LEARN

Activity 2. Optional: Semicolons *(Online)*

Student Guide
Lesson 3: Colons and Hyphens

Can you name the Seven Wonders of the Ancient World, the seven seas, the planets of the solar system, the states of matter? Can you? Did you try? Most people will. There is something about a list that makes the human mind react like a racehorse hearing the starting signal.

People respect lists. Lists are special, so special that they are often introduced by a unique punctuation mark, the colon. And the colon itself is so versatile that it is also used to punctuate three other things: time, the salutation of business letters, and Bible citations.

Another versatile punctuation mark is the hyphen. Hyphens also have several uses. Do you know what they are?

Lesson Objectives

- Identify the rules for dividing words with hyphens.
- Use colons correctly in the time of day, Bible citations, and business letter salutations.
- Use colons correctly with lists in sentences.
- Use colons to introduce long, formal quotations.
- Use hyphens after certain prefixes and before the suffix *-elect*.
- Use hyphens correctly with adjectives.
- Use hyphens correctly with compound nouns.
- Use hyphens to divide words correctly.
- Use hyphens when writing out the numbers *twenty-one* through *ninety-nine*.

PREPARE

Approximate lesson time is 25 minutes.

Materials

For the Student

BK English Language Handbook, Level I - pages L597-L606

Optional

Extra Practice Answers

BK English Language Handbook, Level I - page L600

Keywords and Pronunciation

adjective : a word that modifies, or describes, a noun or pronoun

compound word : two or more words used together as a single word; may be written as one connected word, as separate words, or with hyphens between the words

linking verb : a verb that links the subject with another word that renames or describes the subject

proper adjective : an adjective form of a proper noun; for example, *European* or *Japanese*

proper noun : the name of a particular person, place, thing, or idea; capitalized

LEARN

Activity 1: Colons and Hyphens *(Offline)*

Instructions

A. Uses of Colons

Read about using colons on pages L597-L598. Then do Check Your Understanding on pages L598-L599 and Connect to the Writing Process: Editing on page L599.

Note – For Connect to the Writing Process on page L599, you need not write entire sentences. Just write the word that precedes the correction and the correction.

B. Use of Hyphens to Divide Words

Read about using hyphens to divide words on page L601. Then do Check Your Understanding on page L602.

C. Other Uses of Hyphens

Read about the other uses of hyphens on pages L602-L604. Then do Check Your Understanding on pages L604-L605. Then, use what you have learned to complete Connect to the Writing Process: Editing on page L605.

D. Check Your Work

When you have finished, ask an adult to check your answers to these exercises.

E. Assessment

Go online to take the assessment.

ASSESS

Lesson Assessment: Colons and Hyphens (*Online*)

Follow the directions to take this assessment online.

LEARN

Activity 2. Optional: Colons and Hyphens *(Online)*

Student Guide
Lesson 4: Dashes and Parentheses

Halftime! Some people go to the game just for halftime. There's so much excitement—the bands, the show, the food, and the socializing. At the theater, intermission serves the same purpose (though the refreshments are different). Sometimes people just need or want a break that interrupts the main event.

Halftime and intermissions are both interruptions, but no one minds. In writing, dashes and parentheses are used to punctuate interruptions. Use these punctuation marks properly, and readers may well appreciate the break and the extra effort!

Lesson Objectives

- Use an ellipsis to show a pause or an omission.
- Use dashes to set off a parenthetical expression or an appositive that includes commas.
- Use dashes to set off an abrupt change in thought.
- Use dashes to set off an appositive that begins with an introductory phrase.
- Use parentheses to enclose information not closely related to the meaning of the sentences.

PREPARE

Approximate lesson time is 25 minutes.

Materials

For the Student

- The Ellipsis
- The Ellipsis Answer Key
- BK English Language Handbook, Level I - pages L607-L609

Optional

- Extra Practice Answers
- BK English Language Handbook, Level I - page L611

Keywords and Pronunciation

appositive : a noun or pronoun that identifies or explains another noun or pronoun in the sentence
parenthetical expression : a word or words that interrupt a sentence; for example, *I believe, of course*

LEARN

Activity 1: Dashes and Parentheses *(Offline)*

Instructions

A. Use of Dashes and Parentheses

Read about using dashes and parentheses on pages L607-L608. Then do Check Your Understanding and Connect to the Writing Process: Editing on page L609.

You will also learn how to use the ellipsis to show an omission in a quotation or a pause in a sentence. Print the page and read the information and examples. Then, complete the exercises

B. Check Your Work

When you have finished, ask an adult to check your answers to these exercises.

C. Assessment

Go online to take the assessment.

ASSESS

Lesson Assessment: Dashes and Parentheses (*Online*)

Follow the directions to take this assessment online.

LEARN

Activity 2. Optional: Dashes and Parentheses *(Online)*

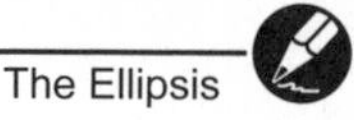

The Ellipsis

An *ellipsis* is a row of three evenly spaced periods: . . .

It is used to indicate that some text is missing from quoted material or to indicate a pause or a break.

Ellipsis to Indicate Omission

Sometimes you only need to use part of a quotation to get your point across. It is acceptable to edit a quotation, but you must indicate that a cut has been made. To indicate where you have made a cut or cuts, use an ellipsis.

> **Original Passage:** The population of Rocksville barely changed at first. In 1880, the population was 1034. In 1890, the population was 1044. In 1900, the population was 1047. In 1910, the population was 1059. And in 1920, the population was 1066. Then, in the early 1920s, the population of Rocksville skyrocketed. By the time of the 1930 census, there were 9,588 people in the town. This was because of a change from farms to factories in the area. In 1880, Rocksville was mostly made up of farms. This was the case in 1890, 1900, and 1910 as well. Most of these were small family farms, passed down from generation to generation. In 1916, the first factories opened in Rocksville. By 1919, there were three more. By 1930, when the population was booming, there were 12 factories in or near Rocksville.

> **Edited Passage:** The population of Rocksville barely changed at first. In 1880, the population was 1034. . . . Then, in the early 1920s, the population of Rocksville skyrocketed. By the time of the 1930 census, there were 9,588 people in the town. This was because of a change from farms to factories in the area. In 1880, Rocksville was mostly made up of farms. . . . By 1930, when the population was booming, there were 12 factories in or near Rocksville.

Sometimes quotations contain *too much* information, and including the full text will bog down your paper and actually make it harder for your reader to understand what you are saying.

Although it is completely acceptable to make edits to a quotation, you *must* use an ellipsis to tell the reader that something has been omitted. Otherwise, you are misquoting the original author.

Tip: If an ellipsis comes after the end of a sentence, you use the period then the ellipsis. This means there will be four periods in a row.

Ellipsis to Indicate a Pause

You can also use an ellipsis in speech or dialogue to show that the speaker is taking a pause or isn't finishing what he or she is saying.

> "I think I remember . . . "

> "We are going to . . . the park! We are going to the park."

The Ellipsis

Rewrite the quotation. Cut the underlined sentences and use an ellipsis to indicate where you have cut.

1. The doctor told Mary that she was going to have to take it easy for two months. She wasn't allowed to run, hike, or climb. She wasn't allowed to jump on the trampoline. If Mary did any strenuous activity, she could break her leg again.

2. I love all kinds of pie! Apple, cherry, pumpkin, blueberry, and raspberry are my favorites. I will eat any pie you put in front of me.

3. The first army approached from the East. Tired and hungry, the soldiers were still ready to fight. The second army came from the West. The soldiers were worn down as well, but they were still prepared for action. The battle commenced at dawn on the morning of August 23.

4. The film was fantastic! The pacing was fast and funny! The actors, very well cast in their parts, were hilarious! Some people may look at the ads and show no interest, but they should give this movie a chance. Everyone should see this movie.

Correct the dialogue below. Rewrite each quotation to add the missing ellipsis to the pauses and incomplete statements.

5. "Diane, I I want to talk to you."

6. "Marcus, what is it? I've never. Why are you. I've never seen you so"

7. "I'll come right out and say it. Will you. I can do this. Will you. Please, Diane, will you pass the salt?"

Student Guide
Lesson 5: Review

In this lesson, you will answer some review questions on what you learned in this unit about other punctuation marks. Before you take the Unit Assessment, this is your chance to find out what you do and don't know about using apostrophes, semicolons, colons, hyphens, dashes, and parentheses. Although these punctuation marks are less common than periods and commas, they are still important in making your meaning clear.

Lesson Objectives

- Distinguish between contractions and possessive personal pronouns.
- Use apostrophes correctly.
- Use colons correctly.
- Use dashes correctly.
- Use hyphens correctly.
- Use parentheses correctly.
- Use semicolons correctly.

PREPARE

Approximate lesson time is 25 minutes.

Materials

For the Student

BK English Language Handbook, Level I - page L612

Optional

Extra Practice Answers

BK English Language Handbook, Level I - pages L616-L617

Keywords and Pronunciation

adjective : a word that modifies, or describes, a noun or pronoun
appositive : a noun or pronoun that identifies or explains another noun or pronoun in the sentence
clause : a group of words that has a subject and a verb
compound sentence : two or more simple sentences, joined by a comma and coordinating conjunction or by a semicolon
compound word : two or more words used together as a single word; may be written as one connected word, as separate words, or with hyphens between the words
conjunctive adverb : adverbs, such as however, used to join independent clauses but also may be used as parenthetical expressions
indefinite pronoun : a pronoun that usually refers to unnamed people or things
independent clause : a clause that can stand alone as a sentence because it expresses a complete idea
linking verb : a verb that links the subject with another word that renames or describes the subject
parenthetical expression : a word or words that interrupt a sentence; for example, *I believe*, *of course*

personal pronoun : a pronoun that varies its form to show the person(s) speaking (first person), the person(s) spoken to (second person), or the person(s) spoken about (third person)
proper adjective : an adjective form of a proper noun; for example, *European* or *Japanese*
proper noun : the name of a particular person, place, thing, or idea; capitalized
transitional word or phrase : word or phrase, such as for example, used to move from one idea to another

---

LEARN

Activity 1: Other Punctuation *(Offline)*

Instructions

A. Review

To prepare for the Unit Assessment, complete Using Punctuation Correctly on page L612 in the *BK English Language Handbook.*

B. Check Your Work

When you have finished, have an adult check your answers. Make sure you understand the corrections for any mistakes you made. If you do that, then you should be ready for the Unit Assessment.

Activity 2. Optional: Other Punctuation *(Offline)*

Instructions

Extra Practice: Complete the Posttest exercise on pages L616-L617.

When you have finished, use the Extra Practice Answers page and check your answers.

Student Guide
Lesson 6: Assessment

Lesson Objectives

- Distinguish between contractions and possessive personal pronouns.
- Use apostrophes correctly.
- Use colons correctly.
- Use dashes correctly.
- Use hyphens correctly.
- Use parentheses correctly.
- Use semicolons correctly.

PREPARE

Approximate lesson time is 25 minutes.

ASSESS

Unit Checkpoint: Other Punctuation (*Online*)

It's time to check what you have learned. Go to the next screen to test your skills.

Student Guide
Lesson 1: Semester Review

Lesson Objectives

- Demonstrate mastery of important knowledge and skills learned in this semester.

PREPARE

Approximate lesson time is 25 minutes.

Keywords and Pronunciation

adjective : a word that modifies, or describes, a noun or pronoun
appositive : a noun or pronoun that identifies or explains another noun or pronoun in the sentence
clause : a group of words that has a subject and a verb
compound sentence : two or more simple sentences, joined by a comma and coordinating conjunction or by a semicolon
compound word : two or more words used together as a single word; may be written as one connected word, as separate words, or with hyphens between the words
conjunctive adverb : adverbs, such as however, used to join independent clauses but also may be used as parenthetical expressions
indefinite pronoun : a pronoun that usually refers to unnamed people or things
independent clause : a clause that can stand alone as a sentence because it expresses a complete idea
linking verb : a verb that links the subject with another word that renames or describes the subject
parenthetical expression : a word or words that interrupt a sentence; for example, *I believe, of course*
personal pronoun : a pronoun that varies its form to show the person(s) speaking (first person), the person(s) spoken to (second person), or the person(s) spoken about (third person)
proper adjective : an adjective form of a proper noun; for example, *European* or *Japanese*
proper noun : Names a special person, place, or thing. Each proper noun begins with a capital letter.
transitional word or phrase : word or phrase, such as for example, used to move from one idea to another

---

LEARN

Activity 1: Review - Round 1 *(Online)*

Activity 2: Review - Round 2 *(Online)*

Student Guide
Lesson 2: Semester Assessment

Lesson Objectives

- Distinguish between direct and indirect quotations.
- Distinguish between possessive pronouns and contractions.
- Distinguish between sentences with clear and unclear, missing, or confusing antecedents.
- Identify and use pronouns correctly in sentences.
- Identify logical and illogical comparisons.
- Paragraph dialogue correctly.
- Recognize and use correct capitalization.
- Use apostrophes correctly.
- Use capitalization, commas, and end marks correctly in direct quotations and dialogue.
- Use colons correctly.
- Use dashes and parentheses correctly.
- Use end marks and commas correctly.
- Use hyphens correctly.
- Use italics (underlining) and quotation marks correctly.
- Use negative words correctly in sentences.
- Use pronouns that agree with their antecedents in sentences.
- Use semicolons correctly.
- Use single quotation marks correctly.
- Use the correct form of adjectives and adverbs in sentences.
- Use verbs that agree in number with their subjects.

PREPARE

Approximate lesson time is 25 minutes.

ASSESS

Semester Assessment: Semester 2 Review and Assessment (*Online*)

It's time to check what you have learned. Go to the next screen to test your skills.